Forward Upward Onw

Life lessons ᵢ ₘ 48 mountains about discipline, determination, goals, habits, mindfulness, character, and confidence.

By Matt Landry

Also written by Matt Landry:

LEARNING TO BE
HUMAN AGAIN

DO YOU REMEMBER WHO YOU WERE,
BEFORE THE WORLD TOLD YOU WHO YOU
SHOULD BE?

www.mattlandry.com

About Me and the 48 by 50 Goal

"You have been assigned this mountain to show others it can be done." -anonymous

The account of this wonderful journey will have little to do with trail names and conditions, history, or even who I hiked with, but more about discovering what we are made of in the process of achieving a big goal. In this specific case, it happens to be a hiking goal. For you, it could be any goal.

First off, I'm not a goals guy. I never used to be anyway. Goals to me were the total loss of freedom. I viewed goals as those things that got in the way when I felt like doing something else. I always felt bad for people who were so focused on their path and completion of a self-imposed challenge. I felt that they missed out on much of life. It turns out, and most of you have probably figured this out already, that discipline and goal setting is actually the best way to have freedom in the long term. Discipline and persistence toward a final result not only builds the character you need so much in life but also provide you with a sense of confidence and more importantly, purpose.

I'll talk a lot about discipline, tenacity, attitude, and mindset in this book. I think they are four critical elements in undertaking any challenge or hurdle in life that may come our way. With this specific hiking goal, those principles are what carried me through the toughest and hardest moments I encountered.

There are a lot of goals we can strive to finish or achieve in life. We all have different ones. They can range anywhere from material items, status in our jobs or life, or personal successes in how we want to better ourselves from yesterday. There are sports and athletic goals, travel goals, and spousal and relationship goals. There are simply far too many to list here because there are as many goals as there are people in the world, and then some.

I've hiked almost all of my life. I was blessed to have a modest mountain practically in my backyard growing up, Mt. Wachusett in North Central Massachusetts. As a family, we would also do the almost required hike up the world famous Mt. Monadnock in Southern New Hampshire every year, just to say we did it. I've had the pleasure of hiking some of the Rockies in Colorado, deserts in Utah, national parks in California, and the Adirondacks in New York. My hiking, though, what I would consider serious hiking anyway, has been mostly in the White Mountains of New Hampshire. This is because of their proximity to me and because I still view them as having some of the most beautiful scenery in the United States.

There are quite a variety of hiking goals and lists that could be achieved in New Hampshire alone. There's the fifty-two with a view list, which consists of all the fifty-two non-four thousand-foot peaks in New Hampshire that offer a view. If you expand the area a bit, you have the sixty-seven New England four-thousand-footers, which encompass several states in New England, some of which are unmarked and have no trail to the summit. If you wanted to take that list one step further, you'd find the one hundred highest peaks in the entire New England area.

Then there are the classic forty-eight four-thousand-footers of New Hampshire. That's the one most seem to know, and the one most have asked if I had done.

Had I done them up to that point? No. How many had I done? I didn't know. I never kept track. My purpose for hiking, up to that time in my life, hadn't been the conquering of any lists; it had just been to simply enjoy the ride (so to speak). I had done a lot of them. I'd done a lot of them more than once. I never really got that itch to do all forty-eight though, neatly checking them off a list as I went merrily along.

I also never refused a hike because I had already done a specific peak. Many friends going after their forty-eight peaks would rather have hiked elsewhere to bag another unchecked mountain than to enjoy one they had done before. I always thought that way of thinking was odd. A good hike on any peak, even if you had hiked it already, with great people is just that, a good hike, list or no list.

I guess some things present themselves at certain times for unknown reasons, and this is no exception. Mid-life crisis maybe? I don't know. I guess we all get reflective of what we've accomplished or haven't at some point in our lives. The concept of doing all forty-eight, four-thousand-foot peaks start to finish by the time I had turned fifty years old on December 19th, 2017 had come to me a few years ago, and just hit me as the right thing to do. It just felt true. Sometimes, we just need to listen to our gut and go with that instinct.

As I mentioned, I've climbed many of these, but never really kept track. For this personalized goal, I decided to start fresh, as though I had never hiked any of them before. Clean slate. You'll hear me think back on some of these mountains with a former fondness of four-thousand-footers hiked previously. Most of these were attempted for the first time. Numerous ones I had hiked; several I don't remember climbing the first time. So, for all memory lapses considered, it kind of was my first time up some of these, if you want to look at it that way.

I hope hikers and non-hikers alike will get something positive out of this book. I also hope it encourages those who have never hiked, to maybe give it a try (just please don't do it unprepared in late May doing the Lincoln/Lafayette loop, as you'll read about in the next chapter).

Thanks for coming along for the hike and the journey with me. I hope you enjoy it.

How All This Wonderful Foolishness Started

Two separate people had died not far from the Mt. Lafayette summit only three weeks before. One slipped off the trail over a steep ravine, the other tried to hunker down out of a storm's way and simply froze to death. I'm glad we didn't know that coming into the hike, then again, maybe we should have known for our own safety.

It was turning into a mild spring, no cold that the record books would speak of in years to come, but there was still a chill in the air, especially at night. Each Memorial Day weekend, my friends Shaun and Sarah, along with myself in tow made our annual camping pilgrimage to the White Mountain National Forest in New Hampshire to safely enjoy what we considered the great outdoors. We had tented the evening before, and except for cold noses in the morning, the sleeping bags had kept us relatively toasty through the night. Thanks to Shaun, being the ambitious early riser that morning, Sarah and I got up about the same time to the smell of fresh coffee Shaun had percolating on the propane-fueled camp stove.

As the caffeine was readily consumed and started to work its magic, we began to make plans for the day. Shaun casually mentioned there was a hike that began right at the campground with a waterfall involved. The trail was aptly named Falling Waters. Nothing too hard, just hike there, take photos of the pretty waterfall, and hike back sort of thing. I approved without hesitation and Sarah cheerfully agreed as well. Plans were made for the early part of the day, just like that. Shaun and I had dabbled with a little hiking at that point, local trails around our houses, an hour or two in the woods. Nothing a water bottle and a Snickers bar wouldn't suffice to keep us alive.

Shaun had been my best friend since we were kids, probably fifteen years at that point. He was a very friendly, cheerful guy who loved to tell a joke. Always smiling. He was always there if you ever needed anything, and about as spontaneous a person as you'd ever meet. Sarah was no different in that regard. Excellent company and always ready to do something fun. Shaun was dating Sarah at the time, and it was no great surprise when they became happily married a few years later.

When we were twenty-two years old, Shaun and I decided to drive across the United States. For the most part, it was a spur-of-the-moment decision. No real, actual planning was involved. We both secured a few weeks off from work and decided that the Rocky Mountains, Graceland, and Las Vegas were calling us, and, of course, we needed to heed that call.

I can still fondly recall packing the car to the point when the back tires looked as though they were going to pop from the weight. We filled it with lawn chairs, a bag of potatoes, and a tent we fully intended to use, but never did. We took along a large wooden contraption that Shaun and I had devised, that came to be known as "the camp box." It was a box that held utensils, about twenty cans of soup, a dishpan, and whole array of other items that were relatively useless. It was literally about as big as a coffin, and it probably weighed about the same too.

The afternoon we left on the big road trip, I started to pull out of his driveway and turned to Shaun. "Which way are we going by the way?" I asked. "I don't know. That way I guess," Shaun replied, pointing his finger down one side of the street, and off we went.

We started on the hike late morning. It was near the end of May, and the sun was starting to get stronger that time of year. I changed into shorts just before we left, and grabbed a cotton hooded sweatshirt, just in case the shaded forest was cooler on the trail. We quickly gathered up a few things to keep us going for the short walk. A few water bottles, about a quart each, some light snacks, and a camera. Keep in mind, this was at a time long before cell phones or Internet, so word of mouth was all we had to go by for hiking or any trail information on that day. In this case, for this particular hike, we'd simply noticed the trailhead sign and asked a ranger about the waterfall.

The trail was pleasant. The air was cool and

refreshingly brisk. As we made our way about an hour out, I remember thinking *I could hike all day in weather like this*. We arrived at the falls uneventfully. There was a small gathering of people; for some, it was a turning around point for the casual day hikers, the falls being the main attraction and final destination for them, just as we had planned for that day. The trail did continue though, to reach some peaks and parts of the much larger Appalachian Trail that encompasses an area from Georgia to Maine.

We took several pictures of the falls and made mention of the appropriately named Falling Waters trail that we were on to a few other fellow walkers, who were ready to head back to camp, just as we intended to as well.

"Hey," Shaun said, "do you want to continue on? Go further up the trail?"

"Yeah, I could do some more," I confidently replied. Sarah excitedly agreed. It was too nice a day not to enjoy the outdoors a bit more. It had been a long, snowy winter, and the warm sun felt like a gift that couldn't go to waste. We started further up the trail with an added bounce in our steps from the new, last-minute, altered plans we had made.

The trail continued on to Little Haystack, and would stretch past to Mt. Lincoln, then Mt. Lafayette. two of the forty-eight four-thousand-foot mountains in New Hampshire, each frequently called a four-thousand-footer or simply a 4k by those in the Northeast hiking world.

As we plugged and plodded away at the trail, we quickly noticed a few different features that we hadn't seen on our hike up to the falls. For one, there were fewer people, and the select folks we did see were carrying larger overstuffed backpacks and more substantial outerwear. We also started to notice that those limited amount of individuals were looking at us as though we didn't belong there, and, I assure you, we didn't. Most of them had what looked like five thousand dollars of equipment on their backs, the best clothes LL Bean and Northface had to offer, and seemingly a week's worth of food and water on them. We, however, had our simple Old Navy attire, complete with cotton hooded sweatshirts, sneakers, short pants, and bottled spring water in hand. Not even a backpack. The last differing detail that quickly came to our attention that wasn't anticipated was snow on the trail. Lots of it, as a matter of fact.

Although the weather was still brisk, the snow that had accumulated over the rough winter had disappeared everywhere else. There was no snow at my house back in Massachusetts or even the campground where we were staying. The roads, my backyard, anywhere for that matter. I mistakenly assumed the peaks of the White Mountains wouldn't have snow any either. I was very wrong in that assumption.

As we trudged our way up to the summit of Little Haystack, the snow got deeper and deeper. We didn't notice how deep because it was well packed from the previous brave souls who had forged ahead of us throughout the entire winter (I learned later the term for this packed snow trail is called a monorail). We actually thought the trees were just getting smaller. "Must be the mountain air," Shaun joked. At one point, I decided to drive my walking stick into the softer untrodden snow just off the trail to see how deep it was. Shaun and Sarah looked at me with a playful grin as I prepared to drive the stick in to see the snow's depth.

I think we expected about a foot or so to be the final result of the impromptu experiment. I stand about five-foot eight, and the stick was about shoulder length to me. I raised the walking stick about two feet above the white surface and forced it down with one quick motion. The stick disappeared. The smiles slowly faded from our faces.

"Wow," Shaun said.

"I know, a little deeper than I thought," I replied.

We didn't expect it to be quite so deep, and we still had the last push before we even reached the summit. We had hiked just under three hours up to that point and decided we may want to revisit our plans for reaching the peak, which we knew wasn't that far away at that point because we could see glimpses of the summit from where we stood.

"I think we should continue," I said. "How much worse can it get?" We all agreed that turning back would be a major disappointment; we had come so far at that point. So, we pressed on, knowing that we had been much farther than the amount we had left to officially summit the peak, but not actually knowing what lay ahead of us, or how far we truly had to go. We felt as if we shouldn't be doing it, but the sense of excitement in our unanticipated climb was too great.

As we slowly lumbered up the last stretch of the trail toward the summit, we were above tree line in an alpine region, and the view was spectacular. The snow was also starting to dissipate because the high winds blow a vast majority of the snowpack off the tops of taller, open peaks into the notches and valleys below. It often doesn't have a chance to settle in.

The general mood was still good, but rapidly declining, and I knew reaching the summit would brighten our spirits. The views up to that point were already worth the effort, so I assumed the peak would certainly be a morale-building climax.

We reached the summit with a few shouts of triumph and exhaustion. The view was life-changing. The Lincoln-Lafayette loop is often voted one of the best hikes in the United States, if not the World. More than one person has certainly gotten permanently hooked on hiking after completing it.

There was an incredible ridgeline of mountain peaks one after the other we couldn't see on the climb up, but they were clearly visible and the trail continued over them, one after another. From where we stood, they didn't look very far apart. The next peak was Mt. Lincoln, and the one after that was Mt. Lafayette. We could see off in the distance that Mt. Lafayette had a ridgeline trail heading back in the direction to the campground where we were staying, quite a distance away, but it certainly didn't look unachievable.

We verified the trail destination with a fellow hiker we bumped into on the summit.

"We're on the Appalachian Trail right now, and it runs past Mt. Lafayette, and that side trail down the steep ridge takes you back to the Lafayette campground. By the way, you guys really don't look like you're very well prepared to be up here, no offense" he added. "Someone died up here a couple of weeks ago. Got caught in a storm and froze to death."

With those words, our eyes became a little bigger. He had certainly gotten our attention. "Thanks" I replied. It was at that moment that an actual feeling of danger, I mean real danger overtook us. *What the hell are we doing up here*? I thought. It was beginning to dawn on us that we might be in this over our heads. Our water had just run out, and we had just eaten the last of our food moments ago. It was sinking in that we needed to get back not only before it got dark, but also before the temperature started to plummet.

We managed to keep plugging away, exhausted. Our physical energy sank from the exertion needed to keep struggling gravity continuing our climb, and fighting the colder air starting to creep in on us. It was going to get dark soon, and we had no light source with us. Needless to say, the other two peaks necessary to continue our journey were much farther away than they looked.

After the climb over Lincoln, we finally reached Mt. Lafayette, with far less fanfare than our first peak. We were tired, we were thirsty, we were hungry, we were cold, and we were getting scared. Our mood was somber, and we knew we still had about two solid hours of hiking to go to finish the trip from what seemed like hell.

As we started our final descent, Shaun and Sarah started bickering. Then it escalated into a full out shouting match. *This ought to be a fun trip down,* I thought. Our legs were wobbling and shaking uncontrollably from the exertion of climbing. Our knees were knocking together, and we were miserable.

At that point, a strange calmness came over me. I don't know why. I looked back over my shoulder to admire what we had accomplished and the distance we had hiked that afternoon, unplanned, and was simply amazed. We had walked almost seven miles of rugged terrain, often on five feet of packed snow, in sneakers and shorts, nonetheless. I turned to my two miserable companions with an almost boyish grin and said, "we don't have far to go compared to how far we've hiked already. Check it out; see that peak back over there? That's Little Haystack way back there, and we can't even see the distance we climbed up to get to that point. We really haven't got that far to go, we can do this. No more uphill, either. All downhill from here."

I wasn't pondering it at the time, but I do remember thinking sometime afterward, that occasionally, you have to look back at where you've been in order to appreciate how far you've come. It's important to concentrate on the destination, but you can't forget the progress you've made either. I also remembered thinking that life has to be risked and you need to come out of your comfort zone sometimes to appreciate its possibilities.

We all stood for a moment admiring the distance we had come, then dusted ourselves off and carried on. As we started the descent, something unexpected came into sight. A sort of large, rustic old house on the mountain, which seemed to be in the middle of nowhere, settled in a little off the trail. As we approached it, it occurred to us that it was a public hut, Greenleaf hut to be exact, put there and operated by the Appalachian Mountain Club. We headed down as quickly as we could and discovered they offered potable water, and we took full advantage, drinking until we almost became sick.

We were also offered a bite to eat from a few of the gracious hikers staying overnight there. We debated staying the night as well, but decided against it, knowing we didn't have much further to go in order to return back at camp.

With elevated spirits, we left the hut and knew that we were going to be okay. We would make it down safely, but just had to beat the darkness and our exhaustion. We managed to slide down a good part of the rest of the hike on our behinds, like little kids sledding on a hill, making great time, and sore, cold asses. We arrived safely back at camp in the dark exhausted and famished.

We all took an oath that we would never do a hike like that again. No more four-thousand-footers. Ever.

Two years later, we did the same hike, but better equipped, and still at the last minute. This time though, we were very well prepared, and had done our homework. We had learned our lessons. I was hooked. The hiking bug had bitten me hard.

The 4,000 Footers

(In alphabetical Order, Followed by Their Elevation in Feet)

Mount Adams	5,774
Mount Bond	4,698
Bondcliff	4,265
Mount Bond, West Peak	4,540
Mount Cabot	4,170
Cannon Mountain	4,100
Mount Carrigain	4,700
Carter Dome	4,832
Carter, Middle	4,610
Carter, South	4,430
Mount Eisenhower	4,780
Mount Field	4,340
Mount Flume	4,328
Galehead	4,024
Mount Garfield	4,500
Mount Hale	4,054
Mount Hancock	4,420
Mount Hancock, South Peak	4,319
Mount Isolation	4,004
Mount Jackson	4,052
Mount Jefferson	5,712
Mount Kinsman, North Peak	4,293
Mount Kinsman, South Peak	4,358
Mount Lafayette	5,260
Mount Liberty	4,459
Mount Lincoln	5,089

Mount Madison	5,367
Mount Monroe	5,384
Mount Moosilauke	4,802
Mount Moriah	4,049
Mount Osceola	4,340
Mount Osceola, East Peak	4,156
Owl's Head	4,025
Mount Passaconaway	4,043
Mount Pierce [Clinton]	4,310
Mount Tecumseh	4,003
Mount Tom	4,051
Mount Tripyramid, Middle Peak	4,140
Mount Tripyramid, North Peak	4,180
Mount Twin, North Peak	4,761
Mount Twin, South Peak	4,902
Mount Washington	6,288
Mount Waumbek	4,006
Mount Whiteface	4,020
Mount Wildcat	4,422
Mount Wildcat, "D" Peak	4,070
Mount Willey	4,285
Zealand Mountain	4,260

The Inconvenience of Discipline

#1 - Mount Garfield

9/4/2014

"If it is important to you, you will find a way. If not, you'll find an excuse." -Unknown

A semi-ambitious hiking goal? What the hell was I thinking?

You mean I have to actually climb the mountains to say I climbed them? To the top? All of them? Really? Are you kidding me? Forty-eight of them? In less than a few years? Who came up with those dumb rules for a goal?

Oh, right. I did...

At the start of 2014, I thought about the New Year and the hope of new goals and challenges it offered, just like many of us do. I also ran into several old arch enemies. You probably know them as well: procrastination, work, discipline, willpower. You know, that whole group. It's always fun and exciting to look over goals and resolutions for the New Year. Make tidy lists with bullet points, and nice headlines that read, "Lose weight, eat right, quit smoking, solve global warming, cure cancer, etc." It's nice to grab that mindset and stand boldly with the greatest intentions of achieving them all and saving the world.

We all have the same mentality at the beginning of the New Year. This is the year I'm going to move mountains, blah, blah, blah. The real truth is that when it comes to actually starting any of it, it's not as much fun as writing those lists. "You mean there's work involved? I gotta wake up early? And drive three hours and hike with a big heavy pack? Sometimes in the mud, snow, or rain?" Blech... These are the kinds of obstacles when presented to us, we usually go with the classic "I really, really want to get these done. Totally. I'll start next Monday, though. Today's just not the day. Or better yet, the first of next month. That'll be the right time." Sound familiar?

I had spent a lifetime with the "I'll do it tomorrow" mentality, and even worse, the few times I was actually able to start something, when the instantaneous results didn't occur, I gave up. *I've been eating well for like three whole days and haven't lost a pound. Screw this!*

Somebody I know had once referred to this mentality of goal achievement as *the inconvenience of discipline.* I like this title because it denotes exactly what it is. An inconvenience. Nobody wants to wake up early, run five miles, do the sit-ups, or put in the time to practice for hours and hours every day. I'll let you in on a little obvious secret I found out though. It took me a long time to learn what most people already know.

That's what successful people do.

It's how they reach their goals. They know that, sometimes, we need to do things we don't want to do. They go beyond the excuses and call it what it is, an inconvenience. But they still do it. Whatever needs to be done, they do it. If there's no time to do it, they make time to do it. They find time to do it. They sacrifice other things to do it. "It" becomes a top priority, and "it" will get done, come hell or high water.

I was already a few days into getting my ass up some of the smaller hills in preparation for hiking the forty-eight peaks. Waking up early, hiking at night, using days off. And you know what else I'll let you in on? It got easier. It felt better, and I was always glad I made the effort and completed the task.

In this sort of pre-training, I hiked just after a light snow, white frosting all over the trees. I hiked and mindfully took the time to listen to a cold front approaching. Honest to God. Changing from a calm afternoon to the trees suddenly groaning with the increasing wind, and storm front clouds thickening. I hiked at night and saw the beautiful city lights in the distance. I would have missed all of these things had it not been for me saying to myself "Shut up. Just hike. I know it's cold, but you won't die. I know it's dark, but you have a headlamp and the boogie man won't get you. It's hiking, not brain surgery. Get off of the couch, get into your car, and climb that mountain by putting one foot in front of the other over and over again."

Yes, after I had done a longer hike, I was sore from head to toe. Yes, I felt like a ninety-six-year-old man getting out of bed the next morning, and yes it cut into my "me" time. But with each hike, it got better. The pains subsided and weren't as bad after every hike, or when I had crawled out of bed the next morning. It really was worth the time and sacrifice. I felt better both physically and mentally.

The first four-thousand-foot peak I officially chose for this goal was Mt. Garfield. It was ten miles in and out with easy grades and a stunning view from the summit at an elevation of 4,500 feet. It was named after President James Garfield, not the cartoon cat. I headed up early, on a beautiful September day. The last time I had climbed this peak was for a Flags on the Forty-Eight memorial event, almost a year previous exactly.

Flags is an annual memorial climb honoring the victims of 9/11. The weather for that particular hike was miserable. The temperatures on the summit were in the high 30s, and if it wasn't raining, there was a heavy, cold mist. Even well-prepared hiking veterans were shivering, and a few members of the team were bordering on hypothermia. The trail was like a running river and the view from the summit afforded about a foot in front of your hand. The wind blew incessantly and offered no relief to the already totally miserable weather experience. If we weren't there for a higher purpose than ourselves, we would have easily turned back. There's an old sort of cellar hole up there from a previous structure that we spent most of the time hunkered down into, afraid to poke our heads into the driving mist and wind. Did I mention the hike wasn't pleasant? I think you get the picture.

One year later, I almost got sunburned. I summited in a t-shirt, and never thought about removing the jacket from my pack for a minute. Funny the difference a year can make, right? Not just on a hike, but in our lives as well. Have you ever had a miserable season or year? Cold and unsure? Then a year later you look back and it's like you're thinking about a different person and situation altogether. A year can make a big difference. For that matter, a day can also make a big difference. I've often gone to bed worried, and frustrated from the day, only to wake up the next morning refreshed and ready to fight the battle anew.

Takeaway: A particular season of your life isn't necessarily permanent. A lot can change in a year, a month, or even in a day.

Find Your Tribe

#2 - Mount Zealand

9/13/2014

"One can acquire everything in solitude except character." -Stendhal

Flags on the Forty-Eight, as mentioned in the last chapter, is a wonderful memorial event held every year to honor those we lost due to the terror attacks of September 11th, 2001. It involves lots of volunteers, each breaking up into teams, and choosing to climb a specific mountain. An American flag is flown on all forty-eight of the four-thousand-foot peaks. So far, all forty-eight peaks have been covered in the last ten or so years. It can be a moving experience and I had been blessed to be a part of it for six of them. It's a volunteer effort put forth by just a couple of dedicated people, and it attracts a lot of positive attention.

I had participated in the memorial with the same basic group of friends for the last three events. This year, we chose Mt. Zealand... or more like Mt. Zealand chose us, after our first two picks were taken. The first come first served open slots fill up quickly every year when the registration period begins. The "good" mountains always go first.

The hike up to Mt. Zealand is very becoming. The trail itself, especially in the fall, has a beauty that goes beyond any summit views. That's a good thing, because the wooded summit here has no actual views at all. More mountains than you think in the White Mountains don't actually afford a summit view.

The Zealand Trail starts on an easy, winding path, passing through some hardwood forest, revealing the reds, yellows, and oranges so closely associated with New England autumns. It winds through open boardwalk and bog areas, past a pond, streams, and eventually to Zealand Falls hut. The Appalachian Mountain Club (often referred to as AMC) huts are always a great place to stop off. Besides the obvious perks such as hot coffee, or leftover brownies and other various snacks baked earlier in the day, you get to meet and speak to some great folks. Not just the hut caretakers, or croo, as they are affectionately called, but the people who come and go throughout the day. This is where you forge new bonds, get current (and more realistic) trail conditions, and ask the basic questions like "what's your favorite hike so far?" or "What's the best route up Mt. Washington?" The hiking community, much like other folks who enjoy the same hobbies, is a close-knit family. Almost all of the conversations contain the phrase: "Oh, I know him/her too! Sure. Small world."

This hike was no different in that community sense with not only my hiking companions but also the folks we encountered. I went with a great group of people and, as expected, made some new friends. Although, as noted, it seems that everyone in the White Mountains hiking circle seems to be acquainted with each other anyway. The AMC huts were also set up along the infamous Appalachian Trail, so you get to meet lots of folks who, if traveling south to north, are well on their way to completing the 2,181 mile journey from Georgia to Maine. We met several at the summit as we proudly flew our flag, and we exchanged taking photos of each other.

I think that's one of the things about this hiking community that binds it so closely together. Besides the obvious love of nature, we all have a shared camaraderie like the Army. In some ways, those beautiful mountains represent heading into battle. A beautiful and scenic battle, mind you, but still a subtle form of war. Us against the mountains, conquering the summits as we go. It makes for a lot of friends enjoying shared experiences and overcoming planned adversity together. There are also plenty of "remember when we did that peak..." or "That time the skies opened up on us and we had to seek shelter..." stories. Even less memorable hikes seem to have some great stories of some sort associated with them.

You see, your friends, and more importantly, your tribe, make you whole. Let me explain that.

We need the company of others and, more

importantly, the acceptance of a community to feel more complete. Being loved is one of the most important aspects of being a human. There have been countless studies done on acceptance into a community, and they all pretty much come to the same conclusions. Being accepted helps to validate you and makes you feel recognized. When you're accepted, you live longer, feel better emotionally, are physically and mentally healthier, and are more fulfilled.

I'm not religious, but I can completely understand the fellowship and community a church offers. Volunteer work often does the same thing. These are all created communities. In the age of technology, communities are moving online. Although they do offer a different form of companionship, it's important to note that real-life, face-to-face relationships are imperative for your overall well-being.

Being an introvert at heart, I love hiking solo, but also like the companionship of a great group of similar-minded folks to enjoy the hike with. I learn a lot about them, a lot about hiking, and even more about life. The trail offers the community that I crave. I suspect it does for lots of folks.

I was looking forward to hiking with new faces for this 48 by 50 goal. I hoped to create some more "remember that time on Mount..." moments that could be shared. And I did.

I only had forty-six more peaks to go... God help me...

Takeaway: We all have a tribe of people we can turn to, so we can feel validated, loved and accepted. Have you found yours? If not, are you actively looking for one?

What Makes a Person Great?

#3 - Mount Hale

10/9/2014

"Human greatness does not lie in wealth or power, but in character and goodness. People are just people, and all people have faults and shortcomings, but all of us are born with a basic goodness." -Anne Frank

Mount Hale was a wonderful hike for so many reasons. I had the company of a friend I had never done a four-thousand-footer with but had hiked with countless times before. The temperature was wonderfully chilly, and the smell of fallen autumn leaves was in the air. We even got to see a few beautiful snow flurries for the first time that season. The first snowfall in New England seems to make everything so fresh, so magical. Ask a New Englander what they think of the snow in early April, and I suspect you'll get a much different answer. It seemed like fall came and went in a flash. Time also seems to go by in a flash sometimes. I was trying to slow it down and enjoy it. All of it.

This is a mountain that a lot of people turn their noses at. No real connection ridge-wise to anything else. It's a moderately short hike with no views (although rumor has it that there once was a view about fifty years ago, but the trees have since grown in). To me, it's a misunderstood mountain, though.

Much like a lot of these summits, the trail leading up was beautiful. The footing was easy, which made for daydreaming a little easier, and my concentration didn't have to be placed on what rock to step on next.

It's unassuming, but a great peak, which led me to think that the small qualities of a mountain like this are what make it great, so I also got to pondering, in my daydreaming state, what are the little qualities that make a person great?

As with a lot of beliefs I had, I used to have certain preconceived ideas attached to them. In this case, values directly associated with what makes a human great. You know, things like honesty, integrity, and courage. These are still wonderful traits, but I altered my perception a little more to include humility, compassion, and simply being human. Well, mostly on being human.

Great humans are just that: human. We all are jealous, we all get angry, we all get down or sad, and we all get self-absorbed and moody. I think people who are great can see this from an almost detached view, and that's what make them great. They're able to accept the fact that they can see their emotions and work from there. I still embrace the standard values like honesty, integrity, and courage, but my views morphed a bit to include being honest with yourself before honesty with others, everyone having their own version of what's courageous in life, and having integrity in the small things first.

I've gone through depression and some mentally challenging times. I learned that I had to both recognize and deal with my emotions constructively. You need to be able to not only accept that you're human but also take those emotions and embrace them. My healing genuinely started when, instead of pushing sadness away, I was able to look it in the eye and lovingly say, *Hello, dear friend. Thanks for stopping by. What can I learn from you? What is it that you're trying to teach me?* I would then thank sadness for his visit, and he would, in fact, leave. This works for a whole host of emotions. Anger, regret, or even happiness. When we push these emotions away or stuff them down, they often come back with a vengeance, screaming to be heard. To deal with them correctly and constructively, we need to listen. What are they trying to teach us? This, to me, is the ultimate human experience. And, as noted earlier, it is also one of the most admirable qualities a person can have. Embracing your emotions, and being human.

The people I find myself looking up to most are the ones society would often least expect you too. Those are the people who inspire and impress me: the selfless, generous, and simple folks in this life, the ones being comfortable with exactly who and where they are. That's who I want to emulate. That's who I want to be. The most confident people know how to deal with their emotions and are more than willing to wear their vulnerability on their sleeves. In Hollywood, nobody personified this better than Jimmy Stewart. This Christmas, watch "It's a Wonderful Life" with new eyes, and realize that the appeal of his character is his vulnerability. It's his ability to display his emotions and ultimately deal with them. That's why we can connect so closely to the character of George Bailey in the movie.

I didn't think of mountains like Hale as any less than some of the others, I just viewed it a little differently. The viewless summit taught me to enjoy the views on other summits when I got them. The easy footing helped me to appreciate lifting some of the challenge and burden from my feet for a while, and the drive there was relatively easy. I can't say that for many other peaks up there.

Takeaway: What are the little qualities of things that you can be grateful for that help you to fully appreciate other things surrounding your life? What are some qualities you would like to possess, or people would you like to emulate most?

Our Ego Sucks (Sometimes)

#4 - Mount Pierce

12/15/2014

"Earth provides enough to satisfy every man's needs, but not every man's greed" -Gandhi

At an elevation of 4,310 feet, Mount Pierce is considered a smaller four-thousand-footer by 4k standards. We did this on a beautiful, cold winter's day. The snow, fallen from the night before, was magically adhering to the trees like fluffy, thick white frosting. It was like walking through a white-colored tunnel, with tree branches bent down from the weight of the fresh, sticky snow. There was just enough chill in the air to make for a refreshing hike, and enough of a physical challenge to say that you accomplished something. It felt good to push myself a little on this one. The night before, I had a wonderful time with old friends at an annual Christmas party. It was lots of fun. Maybe too much fun, truth be told. With two hours of sleep and a bit of a hangover, I hiked Pierce. It took the help of a friend and a little positive thinking, but it got done. Not gracefully, mind you, but we did it. With a good attitude, I may add, and nobody got hurt.

I tend to run physically hot. I'm not the kind of guy going to the beach in summer and praying for 90-degree weather, I can assure you. As a matter of fact, it really can't get cold enough for me. Seriously. Halfway through the hike, in t-shirt and temperatures in the mid-20 degree range, I was throwing snow on my face to stop the sweating. I couldn't cool off. Did I mention I run hot?

My companion for the hike kept asking, "What the hell is the matter with you?"

"I don't know. I got Canadian blood, I guess" would be my repeated reply. When we finally got out of tree line, and my partner was putting his third layer of clothing on, I was standing in the open wind with steam pouring off me. Just so you don't think I'm completely non-human, I assure you that the chill kicked in very quickly and I soon had my three layers on as well.

The summit was so socked in, and the wind was howling so much, we had almost no idea where we were walking. The views on this summit are some of the better ones in the White Mountains, but none would be seen on this day. When we finally did reach a point that calmed a little in a bit of scrub brush, we met someone who had stopped to adjust their pack. We offered friendly greetings and started to continue on when he asked: "Where are you headed to?"

"Pierce summit" we replied.

"Well, stop walking. This is it," he offered, without even looking up from his pack. Ah, thank goodness for guidance. After our viewless stop, we headed back down, trying to retrace our footprints in the snow to find the main trail again. When we regained the path and were below the tree line, it was as quiet and peaceful as church. The trees of the forest do an excellent job of blocking the wind and sometimes elements. I found out later that several people had turned around that day, because the summit was too dangerous to try in their opinion. It's good to push yourself every now and then, simply for the sake of doing it for yourself and no one else. It's also good to have friends helping to challenge and coach you, to satisfy your curiosity and lust for life. Not to inflate that damn ego of yours.

How and why you push yourself is important. If it's for the building of character, confidence, or even for the benefit of others, then that holds value. If it's simply for the bragging rights, then you may want to rethink your shallow motives.

Our ego sucks. Sometimes, anyway. I'm quite sure there was a wonderful "preservation" reason for it at some time. You know, survival of the fittest, reptile brain kind of thing. But now instead of saber tooth tigers hunting us, and our fighting to stay alive vs. being eaten by them, we're fighting against society, with its weird connotations of fitting in and staying ahead (or just trying to keep up with) the crowds and masses. Our competitive side gets the best of us sometimes, and, occasionally, we need to realize that although it can be healthy, it can also be a very addictive and detrimental attribute to have. I wrote about this in a little more detail in my first book *Learning to Be Human Again* (insert shameless plug here _____). Look it up if you get the chance.

The funny part is that for all the power and influence we give to ego, in reality, it's quite frail. Very scared in fact. Frightened out of its wits. It's almost entirely based on greed and attachments, but it's rarely satisfied and only looks after itself. Ego boosters like flattery and status symbols are like drugs. When you get some, you're in constant need of more. That's hardly a great thing to base your attitude, actions, values, and life upon. Human beings are wonderfully, beautifully, and lovingly made. And we are really, really weird. Honestly. Beautifully weird, mind you, but still strange.

Takeaway: Make sure you carefully set goals to better your character or the world in some fashion, not just your personal ego.

Friends With Benefits

#5 - North Kinsman

4/19/2015

"So long as the memory of certain beloved friends lives in my heart, I shall say that life is good." -
Helen Keller

Late Spring in the White Mountains on a high peak is often much, much different than at the trailhead. I had intentions of bagging both North and South Kinsman on this hike. The advantage to multiple peaks is a ridgeline. A ridge basically connects two or more mountains together, with a sort of a small valley between them. The elevation you may need to gain in climbing a peak could be three thousand feet. This equates to three thousand feet "up." Sometimes, it's done over longer mileages (making for a less steep climb) or a shorter distance (which makes a steeper climb). Once you've done that initial climb of gaining three thousand feet in elevation, the next peak is sometimes only a three to five-hundred-foot elevation gain to get to it. In other words, once you make the initial hard climb, the next peak(s) aren't that bad, and even though you're exhausted, it makes sense to check them off the list while you're up there anyway.

Multiple peak bagging adds mileage to an already long day, but, believe it or not, it's easier in the long run. It's obviously faster as well, as you can check several peaks off the list in one day as opposed to returning multiple trips and heading up different trails for the same purpose over and over again.

For the Kinsmans, we chose a trail called "Fishin' Jimmy." People often refer to this trail as "F*ckin' Jimmy." It's not as though it's the hardest trail up there; it's just what they call a PUD trail – pointless ups and downs. I just talked about elevation gain. When you start at an elevation of one thousand feet at the trailhead and hike to, say, four thousand feet, you'd think of that as gaining three thousand feet in elevation, correct? Well, if you include the hilly nature of some trails over the course of miles to reach certain peaks, you can increase that elevation by up to a thousand feet or more. So, starting at one thousand, and ending up at a final elevation of four thousand feet could actually yield four thousand feet or more of elevation gain in total. When hiking, it's not the mileage that wears you out; it's that elevation. Most folks can walk all day. People run marathons all the time. It's the up that kills you. It's the up that's hard!

On top of what seemed like endless elevation gains, we were postholing. What is postholing? To some in the hiking world, it's a black spot upon humanity itself. Postholing is when you're hiking in deep snow without snowshoes and your foot sinks down over and over again, leaving these holes in your wake. Postholes can be not only frustrating for the person creating them, but it can be downright dangerous for the folks behind you. Picture walking on a dirt road full of endless holes you need to avoid. Now picture that in white and colder. That's postholing. Snowshoeing can be incredibly fun, but it's a tremendous amount of work. It can also be exhausting from carrying your snowshoes on your pack if you don't need them.

For this hike, we did take our shoes, but unfortunately, as the temperatures were warming, and the snow was melting, it was more dangerous to use the shoes than not. On packed, wet snow they can act as sleds, and if anyone has post-holed before you (which someone almost invariably does, and did in this case), snowshoes aren't much good. So, we trudged and post-holed. Only partially postholing maybe once or twice every ten steps, so it was sort of like posthole roulette. The snow was five or six feet deep. That means your leg disappeared down a booby trap up to your crotch with every posthole you made. By the end of the hike, I was about one posthole away from a hip replacement. Going either up or down a mountain that way is both tedious and exhausting. Upon arrival to North Kinsman, South was out of the question. It was for me, anyway. It would have to wait another day.

It had been much too long since I had hiked my last four-thousand-footer. As with many things, sometimes, when you have all the time in the world, you simply put things to do off "until tomorrow." The problem with that is that there are always plenty of tomorrows, or so we think. Funny how they all eventually catch up to you, and you run out of them.

I really needed the help of some folks to get this done. Being a perpetual procrastinator, and quite honestly, concerned about doing some of these peaks and trail alone, I simply needed the assistance and encouragement of others.

All I can say is thank goodness for good friends who not only are willing to be there when they say they will but also will challenge you (and themselves in the process) and are willing to help you step outside of your comfort zone. It's nice to have friends to simply hang around with, but I truly believe a real friend will tell you like it is and not be an enabler to poor habits and living a life below the standards you were meant to live. It's a fine line to walk sometimes, between keeping a friend on track and sounding like a nagging mother or a barking drill sergeant, but I believe it's what a good friendship, along with some other wonderful qualities, should be based upon.

Takeaway: Take a minute and think of the people you call friends. Are they adding quality to your life or just enabling your bad habits? Better yet, are YOU adding to others' lives? Are you challenging those around you to be the best people they can be?

Are you compassionately calling them out on their bullshit?

You Pay Now or You Pay Later - But Sooner or Later, You Have to Pay

#6 - Galehead

7/11/2015

"Do or do not do, there is no try" –Yoda

I had a lot on my mind at this point in my life, and this hike like so many others, was a welcome distraction to all of it. It was a stunning day. Surprisingly cool and extremely comfortable for July. I don't often hike on weekends, it's simply too hectic and busy for me. It brings in a much different crowd of people. Not that anyone should be forbidden from hiking, but these are generally the weekend warriors (much the same as I used to be). They come in droves, wearing flip-flops and jeans, often only carrying just a small bottle of water and a candy bar (much the same as I used to).

On these weekend hikes, I usually clean up the most debris from the trail, and the folks, well, just aren't quite as friendly. I guess you could say they aren't all members of the tribe of the hiking community I described earlier. Today was a pleasant exception, though. Because Galehead is a less-hiked trail and leads to a hut along the way, the people were great. I popped into the Galehead hut on the way up for a cup of coffee and ran into a wonderful family with two kids about nine and twelve years old. They were doing their forty-eight as well and loving all of it. They gleefully went over favorite trails and mountains. It's rare for younger folks like that to have a passion for a thing like this or even mountain hiking in general. It takes tenacity, patience, grit, and will to get up these things, and children sometimes don't always have those on a longer excursion. They're often too busy enjoying the now, or not enjoying the now. Time is a more foreign concept to kids. Summers last forever as do fifty minutes sitting in most classrooms. Not these guys though. They had a genuine sense of play with this whole adventure. A sense of play I lost often during my goal keeping. They also had a focus on the mountain they were on, what they had done, and what it took to finish. As a parent, I can imagine those are hard qualities to instill in a child.

After a few long winter months of non-hiking, I had gotten back on the horse to do this one. It was a 10.2-mile hike that I did surprisingly well. And by well, I mean I didn't die, and I wasn't too sore the next day. I also wanted to hike again soon after, a pretty positive sign in my book. I still had a long way to go to complete the list, and it seemed I was dragging my feet on it.

Life is meant, for the most part, to be lived in joy, in happiness, and with fun. Most people don't laugh enough, and they don't play enough. On the other side of the coin are those who play way *too* much. There are some who take life a little less seriously than they should and suffer the eventual consequences that may bring for the future.

The most successful people are the disciplined ones who realize, sooner or later, you have to pay the piper (so to speak). They're the ones who work hard early for an easier life later. Or as entrepreneur Gary Vaynerchuk so eloquently phrased it, "You need to eat shit for two or three years, so you can eat caviar for the rest of your life." Me? I'm an eventual piper payer... I always have been.

I had been blessed enough to have had the opportunity to take some extended time off over the years. I don't mean this to sound conceited, but I've done things in forty years that most folks wouldn't do in several lifetimes. The price for that though is that I'll probably have to work until I'm seventy-five to pay later for what I wanted to do now. Meanwhile, my friends will be all doing later what I already did earlier, because they paid earlier. They put in their time, invested their money, and advanced their careers. I basically had six months off to complete some goals, get some things done, seriously hike some mountains, and to write the book I always wanted to write. I really didn't do much of any of those.

In all fairness, I did use some of that time well. I traveled a lot and took some of the necessary time to heal myself and slow down. I needed that, and I wouldn't take that back for the world. On the other hand, I might have extended that time and taken advantage of my opportunity a bit far.

I guess the moral of the story here is there are things in life we avoid, that we shun, or put off until later. Educations, job opportunities, hard work at the time it needs to be done, or saving up for your retirement. If you aren't putting the effort in on these things early, it comes back to haunt you. You know, you either pay now, or you pay later, but, sooner or later, you have to pay. I was paying a bit for my hiking goals. I still had a lot to climb and the time was growing shorter to do them in. I put off tomorrow what I could and should have done today.

Takeaway: Make wise choices about when you want to pay, just don't be surprised when you finally have to. At some point, we all do!

Everything Teaches Us a Lesson

#7 - Mount Waumbek

8/7/2015

"We all learn lessons in life. Some stick, some don't. I have always learned more from rejection and failure than from acceptance and success." -Henry Rollins

I had just walked for five hours in the rain up a mountain with no summit view that took me about seven hours total to drive to and from. That makes absolute sense, right? I probably would have skipped it if I didn't promise to honor a previous commitment that I should have also backed out of to begin with.

Mount Waumbek is one of those out of the way four-thousand-footers that need to be done in order to accomplish the forty-eight peaks to their completion. It's a somewhat pleasant hike, not too hard, not too easy. No views from the summit, and, in this case, I did it in the pouring rain. It's a semi-pain in the neck to get to, being one of the Northernmost mountains. In the grand scheme of things, it's no less important than hiking any other four-thousand-footer in the White Mountains. Without it, the goal is incomplete. It's as simple as that.

There can be a lot of small steps and pieces in accomplishing any goal. A lot of them are difficult, many of them are thankless, some are life-changing breakthroughs, and many, like Waumbek, can be tedious and uneventful, but oh so important in its completion. It's a necessary piece of the puzzle to get the job done.

I had skipped too many steps in my goal achievements in the past. I didn't think they would mean much, or thought they weren't important, but they are. All those little moments you don't think add up, do. Some things you just can't skip any of the steps for. They create the grand plan and come together to create a final version of a complete goal, or at least a goal done to your satisfaction.

On this hike, in particular, I felt that I was taken advantage of by another friend. I was put to the test of "how far would I go" after already sticking my neck out, and expending lots of valuable time helping. The result was one less friend about a year after I did this hike. There are givers and takers in life, and if the givers don't put limits upon themselves, the takers will just keep taking. I won't go into details about what happened, but I'm not a big fan of folks who require you to not only jump through hoops on a regular basis for their benefit, or who ramp up those demands occasionally just to make sure they can still snap their fingers and expect you to drop what you're doing over and over again.

That past year, for the first time in my life, I was learning to take care of myself. Not in a self-centered fashion, but in a healthier way. I had chosen better friends and was letting the toxic ones go. In some ways, I had felt like a business that needed to make a profit, firing those who weren't on board with helping me or others improve. I trimmed the fat and hired new, more qualified applicants. Actually, that's a weird comparison, because I'm really not the business-minded type, but you get the analogy.

Just as a mountain like Waumbek is an important element to a bigger goal, your friends are all important elements to who you become as well. There are many elements or steps in achieving a major goal. Don't ignore any of them. When it comes down to it, we are our biggest project and goal that we are working with. We ourselves are the most important thing we can work on.

Takeaway: Don't ignore all the steps needed in accomplishing a goal. Even the little, seemingly insignificant ones. These include important steps such as failure, indecision, and even falling on your face. Learn the lesson and move forward.

Help Whoever You Can, Wherever You Are

#8 - Mount Moosilauke

8/10/2015

"The fun thing about getting older is finding younger people to mentor." -Mike May

Mount Moosilauke was the next on the list. If you're not familiar with this mountain and have no idea how to pronounce it, don't worry. Neither does anyone else.

I've heard it pronounced Moose-a-lock, Moose-a-lock-ee, and Moose-a-loke.

Po-tay-to, Po-tah-to.

It was my second time up this mountain. As noted earlier, as a part of attempting this new goal, I dd a lot of these as repeats. I re-struggled with a lot of these peaks. I re-enjoyed a lot of these peaks. In this case, I completely enjoyed both trips up this particular mountain.

This trek I did with a former employee, who called me out of the blue to hike. I was both surprised, and elated. I must have done something right as a boss I guess. I'm always thrilled when a former employee contacts me for any reason, and this was no exception. I would have the pleasure of him joining me on several peaks in this journey, and he was on a personal journey for himself as well (more on that later).

We did this one with about a twenty percent chance of rain forecasted, which in the White Mountains, equates to about a ninety-seven percent chance of rain. The weather is incredibly unpredictable at times up here, and the conditions on this day didn't disappoint. The entire descent, it rained. Soaking rain. And you know what? As miserable as it could have been or, more accurately, as we could have made it if we had wanted to, it was an enjoyable hike. I think putting ourselves in temporary discomfort is good for us. Sort of that "if it weren't for the bad days, we wouldn't really appreciate the good days" kind of thing. My thoughts all the way down kept coming back to the fresh, dry change of clothes we had waiting back at the car and the nice tall beer and satisfying bite to eat waiting for us after. Beer was a big motivating factor for me on a lot of these peaks. That was the reward for having put up with some of the pain and discomfort we went through, and it made the whole trip that much more enjoyable.

As I became a better leader where I worked in a small farm and garden retail store, I often tried to teach employees about the basics. The small things that added up to be the big things. Simple things like cleaning up after themselves, treating people well, setting others up for success, taking responsibility for themselves, and doing a job to the best of their abilities.

After leaving the position, I realized how much I missed working with people. More importantly, I realized how much I missed helping people directly. I chose to write books as my method of making the world a better place, and writing is a wonderful way to help those who may need it, but direct contact is far more personal, fulfilling, and rewarding. When you write, it's you and a keyboard. There isn't a two-way conversation going on. The direct care of folks made a huge impact on me.

I worked mostly with younger employees, and it was a two-way street. Knowing how confusing your teen years can be, I got to help them through a lot of struggles and questions they had in life. It gave me an enormous sense of purpose. The other side of the coin was how much I got to learn from them as well. Seeing life through the eyes of someone younger always reminds me of how much we like to confuse life as we get older. We keep piling on the stress, the additional income needed, our sense of purpose, etc.

Younger people, although stressed, know that life has a much simpler nature to it than we assign it later. I'm a firm believer in doing what you love, and not just living an existence of working, paying bills, and then dying.

My time working with those younger employees was my purpose personified, and after leaving that job, I felt lost. Not many people can say they enjoyed what they did, but I loved my job. Physical limitations caused me to leave. As noted, it was a farm and garden store, and was a barrage of lifting fifty-, and sometimes one-hundred-pound bags, all day, every day. I did that for almost thirty years. You'd think that I would have gotten the hint after my second hernia, but it was my neck and shoulders telling me "We think we've had enough, thanks. Please stop or we'll keep you up every blessed night and then haunt your days with nagging pain for the rest of your life." It was a convincing argument, and, wisely, I listened.

The funny part was that I didn't always like that job. Do you know what changed that made such an enormous difference? My attitude. The job stayed the same, but I didn't. I realized, at some point, that we can make the world a better place right where we stand, no matter where that is. We can fulfill our purposes wherever we are, with whatever we have.

Takeaway: You can help anyone, anywhere, with whatever you have or whatever you do.

You Can't Speak Italian by Just Buying the Book

#9 - Mount Tecumseh

8/17/2015

"You just put your head down and do the work." - Jeffrey Tambor

Mount Tecumseh was another peak that I'd done before. The first time I ever did it, years ago, I triumphantly celebrated my achievement of reaching the summit, turned around, and came back home.

Unfortunately, I reached what was apparently a false summit, and never actually reached the real peak. I had trudged my way up to a misleading high point.

Aptly named, a false peak is what seems like the high point in the area, with a descent on the other side. I thought I was done, but if I had gone a little further, I would have found it re-ascending to a higher point ahead. Later that week, I re-climbed the damn mountain and begrudgingly, but triumphantly reached the official summit.

I certainly didn't make that mistake this time

around. I also never made that mistake again on any other mountain. I did my research about where the final endpoint was. Like any goal, you should have a designated endpoint with measurable steps and results, so you know when you've really finished.

This was one of the worst days I had on the entire forty-eight peak journey. I really didn't want to climb. My body didn't want to do the work, and my head didn't help by producing a negative outlook on the whole trip. I had originally planned to do another peak, but had a poor night's sleep and woke up a bit later than I had wanted. But I improvised and picked a quicker hike to a closer peak to bang this one out. I grumbled and cursed it the whole time I was hiking it and was one of the few I'd done that was a pretty miserable experience overall, due to a combination of being tired both physically and emotionally. The good news is that I did it and pushed forward to the goal of not only this mountain, but toward the bigger picture goal of all of them.

I had to be cautious not to turn this whole project into some sort of loathsome adventure. That wasn't in my plan here. I didn't mind some sacrifice, but if the cost had been greater than the reward, then it would have been time to reassess.

I will say that a positive aspect of doing it was moving ahead, and doing the work to do so. I had also forged ahead with three peaks in the last seven days. That was good for me. That's something I was proud of. It was real, measurable, actual, tangible progress.

The problem I had, and I suspect a lot of people have, is that you sometimes give yourself the illusion of moving forward without *actually* moving forward. Let me explain. I'm great for buying the books and signing up for the courses. That doesn't make you anything, though, except a bit poorer. You can purchase all the *Learn to Speak Italian* books that you'd like, but they don't do squat if you haven't opened them up and applied the information contained inside, right? Buying a book about speaking Italian doesn't make you speak Italian, just because you own it. So it was nice to see actual forward progress, adding more names of completed peaks. Hiking mountains in my head, or just reading the guidebook descriptions didn't check them off any lists.

We'd all like to think we're something we're not or do something we think we can do, but it takes the actual effort and time to get there. Stop pretending you're going somewhere. Just do the work. Climb the mountain. Read the damn book, and stop pretending you can speak Italian.

Takeaway: When creating a goal or challenging yourself, make sure you know where your endpoint is, create measurable steps, and then DO THE WORK.

There Is No Such Thing as Failure, Only Attempts at Success

#10 - South Kinsman

8/27/2015

"There are no secrets to success. It is the result of preparation, hard work, and learning from failure." -Colin Powell

South Kinsman was finally on the books and I could check it off the list. I say finally because you have to climb North Kinsman first in order to get to the South peak. I had already hiked North Kinsman twice without reaching that elusive South summit. The first attempt was for one of the flags on the forty-eight events. Timing, exhaustion, and poor weather turned us away from South Kinsman on that trip. Attempt number two was posthole hell (See hike #5). Well, I had finally reached it.

In hiking North Kinsman twice, I learned something about the nature of the hike that better prepared me for that climb. My failures in reaching the first two times were not failures. They were excellent learning experiences to boost me forward to the goal of finally reaching the top of South Kinsman. I was also prepared to fail a third time, if that's what it took.

Luckily, it didn't. I now knew what the best route to take was, what the general lay of the land was, and the effort that was going to be needed to secure the South Kinsman summit.

I had started some new business ventures, with the hopes of becoming self-employed soon. Do you know what I was looking forward too almost more than anything with these new adventures?

Failing.

That's right, failing. I know that in stumbling, I could change my direction to make it work. I know that in embracing failure, I could move ahead quicker than if I just tried to forge ahead stubbornly, thinking I had all the answers, and not paying attention to the process it needed to go through. By embracing failure, I could shift gears to put my energy where it needed to be put to make it work. Failing means you're taking risks and doing things probably out of your expertise and comfort zone. That's where the magic happens. That's where growth occurs. That's where you can tread where other people are afraid to go.

I was making progress. In this case, it was because of two past failures in reaching the summit.

I did this one solo and enjoyed it. I enjoyed the physical challenge, the trail, and the people I met along the way, including an Appalachian Trail thru-hiker I had the pleasure of hiking with for a mile or two. He had a few stumbling blocks along the way too, but he adjusted and kept going. So there he was, about two thousand miles later. Hiking. Getting closer to where he needed to be. The goal of hiking the forty-eight was my personal challenge. It was a big deal to me. To some, though it's a drop in the bucket. Two thousand miles? Wow.

Takeaway: Expect to fail. Embrace failure. Mistakes today equal success tomorrow.

Who are the People in Your Neighborhood?

#11 - Mount Eisenhower

9/4/2015

"Weakness of attitude becomes weakness of character." -Albert Einstein

After working with the public in that wonderful little farm and garden retail store for well over twenty-five years, you get to meet and know some nice folks. I hated saying I worked in retail because it wasn't the standard form of retail most of us have come to know. Sure, we got the usual general public, but in this store, it was more like family than customers, and that even included the owners whom I worked for.

I did Mt. Eisenhower with a former customer turned friend. Come to think of it, I also did Hale, North Kinsman, Pierce, Adams, Madison, Liberty, Lafayette, Washington, Monroe, Flume, Lincoln, Owl's Head, Jefferson, and Moosilauke with either a former customer or employee. As noted earlier, I guess you never know where your next friend or acquaintance will come from, or the impact you can have no matter where you work or where you are. It took me almost twenty years in my career at the same place to realize that. Our attitude is key to what we do. Once I adjusted my attitude, the universe opened the floodgates and said, "Here, all this is for you."

Mt. Eisenhower still remains one of my favorite summits, and was my second peak associated with the Presidential Range, which also includes Mt. Washington, the highest peak in the Northeast. Mt. Eisenhower is known for its 360-degree view from the summit, and is considered a moderate hike in the world of four-thousand-footers.

We climbed via Edmand's Path. It's one of the best-laid trails in the White Mountains, in my opinion. This trail and Crawford path, which Edmand's Path connects to, are some of the oldest hiking trails in the United States. This trail had the classic workmanship that you often see in things made many years ago when people took pleasure in their crafts. These were craftsman who took extreme pride in what they did, and it shows, yet, at the same time, doesn't.

If you ever venture to Mt. Eisenhower via Edmand's, notice the stonework along the trail that acts as retaining walls, or the casual switchbacks it offers for a gentler ascent. The craftsmanship doesn't jump out at you, but, then again, it shouldn't. It's a trail in the wilderness meant to be unnoticed. That alone is the mark of great work on the development of a trail.

Undoubtedly, the men who built this worked long hours up the side of a mountain in probably less than stellar living and working conditions. My guess is they also loved what they did, because it's demonstrated in their work.

I keep coming back to mindset and attitude as important lessons learned in this book. But they're so imperative in the attempt of any project, big or small. They also have everything to do with your grit, discipline, tenacity, relationships, career, and a host of other important virtues.

Sometimes it isn't the job or situation that sucks, it's our outlook. Take a moment the next time you feel stuck or unappreciated to see where you may be able to make a difference where you didn't before, or how you can look at the situation differently. Instead of focusing on the negative aspects of your current position, what are you grateful for there? Are you, in fact, not only making yourself miserable but everyone else around you as well? Is your work or production suffering because you refuse to embrace it?

We all know those people who are never happy no matter where they are. It's always somebody else's fault, or "if it only wasn't for _____" (fill in the blank) "I'll be happy when _____" (fill in the blank) "It's not my fault; it's _____ (fill in the blank). Make your mark where you are, and adjust your attitude toward your current situation. I'm not saying there aren't trying times or situations, detrimental to our well-being or growth, that need to be changed or addressed, but see if it isn't something you're causing yourself first. You may be surprised.

Takeaway: Are you miserable because you choose to be? What are you grateful for in your life, job, or relationships?

Do What You Can
With Whatever You Have,
But at Least Do Something
#12 - Mount Tom / #13 - Mount Field
10/2/2015

"With mindfulness, you can establish yourself in the present in order to touch the wonders of life that are available in that moment." -Thich Nhat Hanh

Mount Tom? Check. Mount Field? Check.

It was a beautiful fall day, where the foliage was just starting to turn those brilliant colors of red, orange, and yellow. I remember thinking what an incredibly blessed man I was, having all of this beauty only a few hours away, and, being alone on the trail, in some ways, I was able to have all that beauty for myself.

When I finally arrived at the trailhead, I was lethargic from the early morning start, and thought to myself, *you know, today would be a great day to just drive around a bit and snap some photos. Maybe tackle this hike another day.* Instead of talking myself into the drive around, I bargained with myself to at least try this hike by breaking it into smaller chunks. *If I'm still not up for it after thirty minutes, I'll turn around. Then thirty more minutes*, and so on, and so on. I was basically bargaining to stop waiting for tomorrow to accomplish these because they wouldn't hike themselves.

Many folks who are checking off their 4k lists try to do three summits on this particular hike. Mounts Tom, Field, and Willey. Today I went with the intentions of trying to tackle either two or three peaks, but quite honestly, would have settled for even one. The first thirty minutes were brutal. I was keeping a pace that was too fast for me. I was getting winded. *Slow down* I told myself, *enjoy this*. After slowing my pace slightly, and regrouping my thoughts a little, I was able to physically catch my breath. A big part of hiking to me is trying to enjoy each one, and much of that comes from feeling good physically. After slowing a little, I was able to loosen up a bit. The first half to full mile of a hike is always the toughest to me, leaving me breathless, sore, and sweating. Once I warm up and find my steady pace, there's usually no stopping me.

I don't know how many other times in life I slowed down and found myself getting more done, or simply concentrating on one thing instead of multi-tasking and finding my productivity levels increasing. Besides the productivity aspect, I simply enjoyed the task at hand more. I was more mindful of my surroundings and found myself more grateful for the experiences I was having.

That's the cool thing about being mindful. Being cognizant of your actions is the purpose of being mindful. Does it mean you change your habits overnight? No. Does it mean you become a perfect human? Oh, goodness, no. It means that when your pace is too quick, you notice it and slow it down. It means that when you're not eating well you notice as you're bringing the fork to your mouth and put it back down, replacing it with better nourishment. Being mindful means that when you're angry, stuck in traffic, that you refocus your thoughts to the right place by realizing that getting mad won't do anyone any good. Zero. That's mindfulness in action in helping you to practice better habits. Taking mindfulness to the next level, we begin to notice the chirp of a bird, the sound of a leaf falling, or just feeling the light breeze on our face.

I was glad I decided to give this hike a try. It was a pleasant day in the woods, with some wonderful folks and friendly gray jays along the way. Gray Jays are an anomaly in the mountains. Unafraid of people, these birds freely eat out of your hand. Some would argue against the feeding of wildlife, but I tend, in this case, to lean more toward the "experience being one with nature" aspect they deliver, and deliver they did.

I bagged two summits, and it really dawned on me that all of these hikes, just like life, are all done the same way: mindfully one step at a time. Each one puts you closer, and each one is as important as the last and as important as the next. The same principle applied to my overall goal. I was over the quarter-completed mark. Halfway would come soon. Each mountain comes, one at a time. Each one is completed, one at a time. Slowly, but progressively. Each completed part of the goal builds upon the last, and points toward the completion.

Takeaway: Are you finding the time to slow down, or simply be mindful of everything around you?

The Sun Always Shines Brightly in the Sky

(Even on a Cloudy Day)

#14 - Mount Jefferson

10/6/2015

"With optimism, you look upon the sunny side of things. People say, 'Studs, you're an optimist.' I never said I was an optimist. I have hope because what's the alternative to hope? Despair? If you have despair, you might as well put your head in the oven." -Studs Terkel

I remember taking a short hike that was local to me on an overcast day many years ago and bumping into a father and daughter coming toward me from the opposite direction on the trail. The girl couldn't have been more than nine or ten years old. As we approached each other on the path, we engaged in idle chit-chat. I remember saying something like, "Too bad the sun isn't out today, huh?" The little girl, without missing a beat said, "The sun *is* out. It's just behind the clouds; that's all." The wisdom of children. She was right, too. The sun is always shining, whether we see it or not.

Mt. Jefferson was number fourteen. Slowly, but

surely, these were getting done, this hike was deceiving in many ways though.

The Presidential Range in general, is an extremely rocky, open, and a potentially dangerous area. Part of the range includes Mt. Washington, which is one of Mt. Jefferson's neighbors. Washington is known for its nasty, merciless weather at any given time of the year. So much so that it's often dubbed "the worst weather in the world." It's no joke up there. With Jefferson close to next door, I understood the possibility of bad weather wasn't all that far behind Washington.

In addition to the rough terrain and dangerous, unpredictable weather possibilities, the Caps Ridge trail to the summit of Mt. Jefferson is listed as one of the tougher trails in the White Mountains. Trail guides used words like "steep, rough, slippery, exposed, scrambles, and strenuous."

I learned to respect the mountains a long time ago, especially on my first trip up Lincoln and Lafayette that fateful day in May, wearing nothing but sneakers, a sweatshirt, and shorts slogging through five feet of snow. I also gain added respect for these wild places when I hear about how many people are either injured or killed on them every year. I've since become what I would like to think of as a very experienced and seasoned hiker.

This hike started in the mist. Thick fog and clouds prevented us from seeing more than five feet in front of us at times. Another aspect of the Caps Ridge trail is that it's relatively short, with minimal elevation gain compared to any other trail to reach a Presidential Range peak. The view along the way was also supposed to be stunning. With the fog and mist blanketing us along the trail, we never got to experience that.

In most areas of the Presi's (as the Presidential range mountains are often affectionately called), once you ascend above tree line, the views are spectacular. A misconception about mountains to some, is that as long as there are no obstacles to your line of vision, all views are the same. I would disagree with that. All the views are beautiful in their own way, of course, but some, depending on the outlying terrain, are more spectacular than others. This is true in the Presidential Range. Once you're above tree line, your views are of all the other surrounding mountains, for miles and miles.

I'm not going to lie to you; the idea of this hike scared me. With all of the pre-hike production about its danger and difficulty, I went into "oh shit" mode the night before, and continued into the trailhead that morning.

Like so many times that came before and would follow this hike, I took it slowly, and one step at a time. The tough parts were challenging, but far from impossible. The worst parts were quite doable, truthfully. Something else dawned on me that hadn't before as well. These tough, scary, challenging hikes were also fun. Really fun, to be honest with you. The scariest sections of these hikes turned out to be puzzles of some sort, with your mind figuring out the best route up the slabs of rock, or where the correct placement of your next step would be. You see, hiking can be a lot like chess. You're not always thinking about where your next step will land, but additionally where the next five after that will take you, what foot you should lead off with in order to allow the other foot to be placed correctly, and so on. You're often thinking what your next moves will be.

As we approached about an eighth of a mile from the summit, still socked in the fog, we relegated that there would in fact, be limited visability today. *No chance of a view today,* I thought. Although disappointed, the climb to that point was fun, and view or no view, was well worth the time and effort we put into it for the day. At that moment, I encountered a hiker coming down the trail and cracked a joke something along the lines of "I bet the views were great today, eh?" The hiker, with a widened smile and thick French accent replied, "Simply breathtaking." I couldn't tell he was kidding or not though. "Are you putting me on?" I asked. He very seriously delivered the surprising news that the view was, in fact, gorgeous just ahead. We pressed on, and low and behold, we found ourselves emerging from the interior of the clouds, and were above them on the summit. This is commonly known as an undercast. It's kind of like an overcast day, except the clouds are below you instead of above.

I wonder how many times we almost gave up on something when the payoff was better than we expected and was just around the corner, or in this case, just a little further to climb. Looks at the moment, can be deceiving.

There was an undercast sky on one side of the ridge, and a beautiful, unobstructed view on the other. An undercast gives a very neat feeling of almost being in an airplane with the just the tips of surrounding mountains poking out over the tops of the fluffy white clouds surrounding them. I used the term *fog* to describe the hiking conditions, but hiking in a cloud is probably a more accurate statement.

We decided earlier to come down another route and car-spotted an additional vehicle at a second trailhead to decrease the walk by a few miles. We walked along the Gulfside trail, towards Mt. Washington and the views were spectacular. It's essentially an open ridge hike that connects Jefferson to Washington.

The clouds below were slowly moving up to the top of the ridgeline from the valley below, and when the clouds reached the ridge, they would rise then sink below to the other side of the mountain pass. Nature can act much differently in the mountains, and the results are often things you would never see from below.

We carefully, but methodically rock-hopped down Jewell trail back to an awaiting car back at the trailhead. I was glad we had pushed through this hike, fog and all. It was one of the most memorable I had in the whole journey.

Takeaway: No matter how many clouds you may see around you, the sun is always shining brightly.

Are We There Yet?

#15 - Mount Osceola / #16 - East Osceola

11/3/2015

"If you could kick the person in the pants responsible for most of your trouble, you wouldn't sit for a month." -Theodore Roosevelt

The Oceolas consist of two peaks, Mt. Osceola, and East Osceola. Osceola by itself is one of the most popular because of its southern proximity, making it easier for folks from the Boston area and all other points South to access. It's considered to be one of the easiest to climb, often recommended for someone who may be doing a four-thousand-footer for the first time.

It was an 8.4-mile hike that I honestly couldn't wait to end for a while until I adjusted my attitude a bit, yet, again (I warned you attitude and mindset were imperative pieces to the goal completion). Luckily, I was able to really enjoy some parts of this hike because of that adjustment.

I met a hiking friend along the way I knew from social media and was reminded of the small and caring hiking community in the White Mountains. Once I slowed down, I was able to enjoy the sound of scattering leaves and the crisp smell of fall in the air. I was able to mindfully embrace the light wind on my face, and the sound of red squirrels and birds chirping. I was able to listen to my body and slow down a little to catch my breath (both figuratively and literally). I enjoyed the trip. I enjoyed the journey. I WAS enjoying the journey. I just needed to remind myself of that sometimes.

"Are we there yet?" Can you remember asking your parents that on a road trip? Especially a long trip that had just begun. I have friends (and have done this myself) who after the first mile in on a seven-mile hiking trip, ask the same thing. *Are we almost there yet?* My answer used to involve eye rolling or the classic "Yup, we're almost there, just around the corner" exaggerations for the sake of sanity. Now, I have a different perspective and thus give a different answer. It doesn't matter if we are or aren't. Enjoy the hike/trip/ride. We'll get there eventually, or maybe we won't get there at all if we chose. Whether we complain and stomp our feet sulkingly, or exhibit a great attitude, enjoying whatever trip we're on, it's still the same amount of time or mileage involved. Enjoy it. Savor it.

The ride of life is no different. Why are we always looking forward so much to some sort of final destination? A final stop of some sorts? Enjoy the journey. The good, the bad, the ugly, and the beautiful. Take it as it comes. All of it. It's too short as it is, why are we always focused on "Let's get this over with, so I can move on to the next thing that I can't wait to be over with, so I can move on to..." it can turn into a vicious cycle. You get the point...

Sometimes, we just need to get out of our own way. Actually, we need to do that most times. We certainly can be our own worst enemies, can't we? I was listening to motivational speaker Larry Winget the other day, and he was saying that we're all satisfied because we created exactly where we are in life, almost no matter what the situation, and he's right. We created our circumstances and made the choices to be exactly where we are today. The finances, the relationships, our jobs, and our living conditions, and yes, even our happiness. We chose all of them. We also continue to choose them. We choose how we act and react, what we say, and where and how we'll live. We're all personally accountable for all of it. Really. That may be a bitter pill to swallow, but it's true.

On this hike, I consciously took control and responsibility for my attitude. It was a big turning point for me, not only in this goal but also in my life.

Takeaway: I am responsible for myself, my actions, and my reactions.

Sometimes We Need to Do Things Afraid

#17 - Mount Willey

6/23/2016

"He who is not courageous enough to take risks will accomplish nothing in life." -Muhammad Ali

As mentioned earlier, Mt. Willey is part of a trio of peaks along with Mt. Field and Mt. Tom that most folks usually claim in one trip. After achieving Tom and Field previous in the season, I simply didn't have enough gas to complete Willey along with them on that trip. So it goes. Life presents us with challenges. Some we can conquer and some we simply leave for another day and take a different route to get there.

As with a lot of these hikes, I simply didn't think I could muster up the energy early on in the climb. It was steep right off the bat; I was out of shape and knew I was going to come upon the infamous "ladders." A set of what seemed like a hundred steep, sometimes slippery steps near the end of the hike that would challenge my comfort zone by also having to come down them. They certainly didn't disappoint. Both going up and coming down.

I kept pressing on, and luckily the terrain flattened a bit. The hike quickly went from "probably not" to "I think I can do this one." The steep and challenging finale to the hike wasn't easy, nor was it welcomed, but I trudged on.

Scared to death at the ladders heading up, all I could think about was "this is going to really suck coming down." And, as a lot of our fears seem to try to falsely project, it turned out that it wasn't all that bad. I froze once or twice but kept it in my head to just keep moving, keep going. Stop thinking so much, and act.

These steep sets of ladders were linked by a plank that crossed over the top of one set of stairs to the bottom of the next set. The distance between the two was about three feet, which needed to be skirted across sideways very carefully. Years ago, that may have been a point I would have turned around on, but not that day. I carefully and slowly climbed them. *Not too bad*, I thought. Going up wasn't as bad, because my view was always looking up to where I was going; coming down, I felt like I was looking at where I could be falling. After a few deep breaths, I cautiously stepped down each stair and then held my breath as I skirted the bottom plank to the next. This, more than the summit itself, seemed like the point of victory in this hike. The hike was easy, the ladders, not so much.

It felt extra good to accomplish the ladders and check this mountain off of the list. I had been recently laid up after hernia surgery for a while, and you know, it's funny how you miss what you don't have. A week previous to this, I had hiked Mt. Wachusett, that local smaller mountain in my backyard. It's a hike I had done thousands of times. Because of my surgery, I hadn't hiked in a while but decided to give it a go. As I was chugging up the trail, sweating like my life depended on it, two girls in their twenties who were descending from the summit started giving me the standard "you're almost there! You got this!" pep talk. I had, somehow, suddenly become the old guy trying to climb an easier mountain like it was my first time. "Thanks! Not too far? Do you promise?" I replied, trying not to sound like I hadn't hiked that trail thousands of times before. "Nope. We promise; you're almost there!"

An important lesson my Father taught me was to never take away someone's blessing. Just like we all like to feel good doing or giving something to someone, don't take that away from someone else. When someone grabs the check for lunch, I give a genuine "No, no, we'll split it." If they insist on grabbing the check, I give a warm "Thank you! I really appreciate that!" I've also learned the same with compliments. Give freely, but accept with a heartfelt and humble "Well, thanks. That's a wonderful thing to say. I really appreciate that." It's not for you; it's more for them.

As noted, I hadn't really hiked much prior to the

operation. As soon as somebody told me I couldn't hike, that's when I craved it. That's when I really wanted to do it twice as badly. So goes a lot of life. Don't wait until it's too late. See the sunset, kiss your lover and hike the mountain. Someday, you may not be able to and wish you had and regretted you hadn't.

Takeaways: Is there anything in your life you keep putting off for fear of the results? A difficult conversation or job change maybe? What are your steps? Are you making sure you allow people to give you their generosity and blessings for their benefit, more than yours?

There's an Ice Cream Store at the Top

#18 - Cannon Mountain

7/21/2016

"Before the reward there must be labor. You plant before you harvest. You sow in tears before you reap joy." -Ralph Ransom

After I had gone out of my comfort zone enough times, the challenges of life and of the mountains got easier. Cannon was somewhat of a challenging mountain, but for one of the first times, a good challenge. I mean, it was no harder than any of the other peaks, but on this one I had less anxiety about it. I think that it's because almost anything is hikeable as long as you're careful and take your time. I was in no hurry. I knew if I put one foot in front of the other, I'd get to the summit and back down again in one piece just like I have a hundred times before. Just like thousands of people on that very trail have done before.

A nice, unexpected factor occurred on this hike, it was the bouldery nature of Kinsman Ridge trail. These were giant rocks you simply couldn't step over to get across, these were rocks that needed to be climbed or sat on, and slid forward on, one at a time. I felt like a kid scrambling over the large boulders, slowly and methodically, one at a time. I enjoy myself on a lot of hikes, but fun isn't always a word I'd use to describe some of them. This one was fun.

It was a solitary hike for the most part on the trail. Even though it was the weekend, not many had elected to climb this peak that day. It was a cooler day for July, and the weather was perfect.

I remember hiking with my friends Shaun and Sarah many times after our unprepared Lincoln and Lafayette adventure. As we continued hiking four-thousand-footers, we would joke amongst ourselves to boost each other's spirits when we were feeling tired or just plain exhausted. Many of these lines are classic hiker lies in order to keep people, mostly newer hikers, motivated. For those of you who are hikers, I know you've used them. If you've never hiked, feel free to indulge with any of these if you ever start.

"We're almost there!"

"It's just around that next corner."

"We're (you're) more than halfway now!"

"Can't be much longer now!"

Two other classic lines we used to use on approaching hikers as we were coming down were:

"There's an ice cream store at the top," and "You'll love the bar they have up there. Ice cold beer!"

Most folks we ran into never fell for it, but we'd get an occasional new, wide-eyed hiker who was drooling over the ice cream they would get on the summit. I never knew how many people we probably disappointed, but I bet we got a lot of folks to the summit with a spring in their step though.

As I approached Cannon summit, I was joined by approximately three hundred additional people. You see, Cannon is also a ski area that has a gondola that gives rides to the summit. After making my way through the selfie-taking kids, cigarette-smoking tourists, and folks wandering aimlessly around, I sat down at the Tramway Gift Shop and cafe and had an ice cream, then finished off with an ice-cold beer before my descent.

Takeaway: Rewards can come in unusual places at unexpected times; look for them, enjoy them, and be grateful about them when you can.

Wing It

#19 - Mt. Hancock / #20 - Mt Hancock South

8/27/2016

"Life's journey - it unfolds for you as you are ready for it." -RuPaul

Long before the Internet, there were little ways to do much accurate research on hikes except for guidebooks or word of mouth. I remember doing the Hancocks many years ago, and the only reason we did it was that we asked someone local for a hike close by and they recommended these, because they were right around the corner.

The keyword I remembered from this hike was steep. Steep up and steep down. My memory and the mountains didn't disappoint.

Slowly and steadily I climbed and, just like thousands of times before, I hiked the mountains. The route to hit both peaks forms a loop, which is nice. You get to experience two different trails and two different views that way. Although the summits didn't afford actual views, there were a few lookouts that sufficed in meeting my distant mountain view fix. I'm not a person who times my hikes, in the sense that I need to beat a previous time, or time the book says is average, but on this hike, I beat the book time. For a slow hiker, that's a minor achievement, but more importantly, it meant I was feeling well. The hikes were all going well and getting easier in the sense that I wasn't keeling over, out of breath halfway through them.

I picked another weekend day for these, which was very unusual for me, but I'm glad I did. The folks I met along the way were wonderful, and the hike was about as pleasant as I've ever been on. This was one of those hikes I hadn't really planned to do, but the night before, at the last minute I decided to head up and get them done. I was so glad I did.

There was very little spontaneity in most of these hikes, granted there's a safety factor that involves planning ahead, but that doesn't mean to say you can't prepare well the night before, and then just go for it. I get so busy "planning" my life, I forget to just wing it sometimes. By that, I mean I forget to be spur of the moment. Doing things at the spur of the moment has a great deal to do with a sense of play, not unlike you did when you were a child.

I was getting better at being spontaneous, though. I still had anxiety that rose and fell which directly affected my choices, but I was learning to both take care of my needs and still stretch my comfort zone a little.

When you have anxiety, you try to control your circumstances, and the future. That way you can control life's outcomes. But guess what? It's just an illusion. You really can't control any of it. Life is going to happen however it happens no matter what. Hence, my new attitude on spontaneity. Life is to be embraced at every moment. Even the unplanned ones. *Especially* the unplanned ones.

Takeaway: You can try to direct parts of your life to go a certain way, but ultimately, you can't control life.

Forward, Upward, Onward

21 - Mount Flume

9/1/2016

It's up to each individual to do the best they can given the life they have, rather than regret the one they don't. —Arlo Guthrie

This was the second peak I summited with Chris, a former employee turned friend. The original plan was Mt. Washington, but the weather refused to cooperate. Some hikes are better suited for rainy days, and some simply aren't. We opted to summit Flume via the Osseo trail, off of the Lincoln woods trail due to its gentle footing and less muddy path. People often don't realize how dangerous hiking on wet rock can be, sometimes making the climb more treacherous than walking on ice. Mt. Washington, along with its unpredictable weather, is a heap of strewn rocks for a majority of the hike, leading to an increased chance of a slip or fall when they get wet. We made the right choice tackling Flume.

With rain upon us, we cheerfully headed up Osseo. I love hiking with people who don't mind getting a little wet or dirty. Some of us even relish the thought. There's something to be said about making ourselves physically uncomfortable and delaying our gratifications for the benefit of becoming better people.

True hikers fall into this category, trudging their way in all kinds of weather to reach their destination. Most successful people also fall into this category, never afraid of diving into a challenge, headfirst.

You find lots of things translate from the trail to real life after a few "uncomfortable" treks. Specifically, you tend to appreciate what you have more, complain less, and savor the little things and comforts you may have taken for granted before. There's no better feeling than putting on a fresh, dry shirt or socks after a wet hike. Or a nice cold beer at the post-hike meal. They all rank up there with opening presents on Christmas morning when you were a kid, or getting your first kiss. Next time it rains, go for a nice long hike and then change your shirt and socks to see for yourself.

One thing I know is that we were not turning back, and if I had suggested hiking Mt. Everest in the dead of Winter, Chris would have been there to charge up to the top. That's the cool thing about him, his tenacity and resilience. I admire people like him because even when life throws them curveball after curveball, they roll with it. It may not always be easy, but they press on. They're the poster children for the phrase "Forward, Upward, Onward."

Chris' dad passed away when Chris was working for

me at Agway, the farm store. Chris was just nineteen years old, and his dad was only fifty-two. Chris' Father had Huntington's disease, a potentially hereditary neurological condition that Chris has a fifty percent chance of inheriting himself. His Grandfather passed away from the same affliction, and his sisters have the same odds of getting it themselves. The disease not only shortens your lifespan but also adversely affects your co-ordination and brain as it progresses. You can get tested to see if you have it, but Chris opted not to for the time being. Regardless, the condition, if you inherited it, usually reveals itself when you get to about forty years old.

For as well as Chris handled his potential future burden, the loss of his Dad still affected him deeply. It's tough to lose a parent that young, but it's also hard to see them suffer in any capacity, especially when you're only fourteen or fifteen years old.

I prided myself on being a good listener with the ability to distribute empathy and fair advice, but this one was a tough one for me because it's something I had simply never gone through. I had no experience or reference point dealing with something of this nature.

The only person I knew who had gone through a similar experience was Arlo Guthrie, the folk singer (remember Woodstock and Alice's Restaurant?). You see, that's what Arlo's Dad, legendary singer and songwriter Woody Guthrie (This Land Is Your

Land) died of. I had heard that Arlo never got tested himself. He also had about a fifty percent chance of inheriting the gene too. On the off chance I could help Chris in some way, I attempted to contact Arlo, and he graciously replied with a beautiful letter.

Here's part of the letter Arlo wrote:

> *"I've never been tested. But, I'm not scared or angry in general, so it's hard to give advice to someone who may be so inclined. It is a choice one makes regardless of circumstances (otherwise it don't mean much). I take each day at a time, and am generally thankful. Having a life cut short of expectations is a difficult reality, but look what my Dad did with the life he had! It's up to each individual to do the best they can given the life they have, rather than regret the one they don't."*

Great advice, whether we're facing a potential disease or not. Chris carries on every day, just like the last. He's learning to manage the unknown, and he's maturing well. Maybe one day he'll get tested when he's ready. These are the kinds of things that build not only character but also resilience. It also proves that everyone is fighting a battle most other folks will never know about. If you met Chris, you'd never know what was going on behind the scenes in his life. He's never asked for sympathy nor has he exhibited any need to do so. Does he still wonder what the future will bring? Of course he does, he's human. Can he change the outcome of the prognosis? No. So, Chris is learning to accept that part of his life in order the change the things he can change, and let go of the rest. That's not always an easy thing to do, but it's an important lesson in freeing up your energy to be put in better places.

I once heard an old saying that if you wrote all of your troubles down on a piece of paper and put it into a bowl with hundreds of other pieces of paper that others had written their troubles on, and you pulled one out at random, you'd probably want your troubles back again.

Takeaway: It's up to each individual to do the best they can given the life they have, rather than regret the one they don't. Change the things you can change, and let the things you have no control over go.

Courage Over Comfort

#22 - Mount Carrigain

9/11/2016

"This is no time for ease and comfort. It is time to dare and endure." -Winston Churchill

The annual flags on the forty-eight 9/11 memorial event is something I look forward to every year. Although commemorating a horrific event in our history, it's almost always a positive experience for me and most of the other participants on many different levels. I always meet new people and encounter old friends I may not see for the rest of the year.

Because it's a rain or shine event, we also hike no matter what the circumstances generally bring (within the safety guidelines of the group, of course). That means that we're forced (in a good way) to hike no matter the conditions, and that's a good push to remind me that all days aren't perfect, but we still need to press on. No different than in life, I guess.

One of the reasons I participate in the event (besides the obvious hiking aspect) is that I knew someone who died on that tragic day. He was a customer of mine at the farm store I managed. A quiet farmer who often came in with his Father or Mother to buy the little pressed paper berry baskets during the raspberry or blueberry harvest season.

Always a bright smile, and always a kind word. I didn't know him well, but we knew each other on a first name basis, and I always respected him both as a person and as a farmer. Farming isn't an easy life. The only aspect of our relationship was the farm store, and I only knew him from that reference point.

He fooled me, though. Or maybe I fooled myself. This simple farmer was one of the pilots of the planes that went down. His name was John Ogonowski. I was later to find out that his parents did, in fact, still farm full time. John farmed the land that he grew up on part-time, not needing to do it full-time, as he made excellent wages as a pilot. It's what he did with that small patch of land that really spoke to the testament of the man he really was. He gave away all the food he grew to shelters and the homeless.

That day, on 9/11, I heard them announce his name on television, complete with picture, and I was in shock. Absolute and utter shock. I was already angry at the audacity of an attack on the United States. After I heard his full story about his generous nature, I became angrier. He was a hero long before 9/11. Now he was gone needlessly.

I thought of the discomfort that the people of 9/11

had to endure, the discomfort of the men and women who were police or firefighters. I thought of the discomfort of the brave and scared souls flying on the planes, and yes, the discomfort of John Ogonowski flying that plane, under those circumstances.

We chose Mt. Carrigain through the flags on the forty-eight lottery. After a few viewless and second choice mountains, we got a good mountain for the event. Wooded summit in case of strong winds, but a tower on top for stunning views. We chose the mountain a full month before the hike, so predicting weather is impossible. Getting a mountain that isn't as exposed can actually be a very good choice, depending on the day. I think back to the cellar hole we had on Garfield and the shelter of North Kinsman the year before that in similar rainy and windy conditions. I felt bad for the open summited folks those years, fully exposed to the winds and rain.

We camped the evening before, so were able to hit the trail early the next day. They had predicted thunderstorms, which aren't unusual in the White Mountains in summer but were unusual for the middle of September, and in the morning hours to boot.

Thunderstorms are one of the only reasons I would cancel a 9/11 hike, or any hike for that matter, especially if there's an open summit or ridge involved. Add in the fact we were carrying metal flag poles, and we suddenly became potential human lightning rods.

Judging the radar in this scenario, we opted to go ahead with the hike. Worse case, the thunder would pass early, while we were still well below the summit in thick tree cover, and we also could turn around and retreat, if need be.

As we pressed on, the skies opened up wide. The rain came down heavy, and the thunder rumbled hard in the distance. Knowing the potential weather circumstances of the day, we were well prepared with rain shells, waterproof boots, and a packed change of clothing for the summit. The trail slowly became muddy, and the sound of the rain pelting against our rain hoods was deafening. Although we may have been wet, our spirits weren't dampened. We continued on. And, just as quickly as it had appeared, the storm passed. Upon its exit, we were left with a stunning day, complete with bright sun and just enough wind to fly the flag proudly on the tower.

I've mentioned this before. Don't be afraid to endure discomfort sometimes. The rewards are far greater in the end for those who do. Avoiding all the things in life that we don't like will never move us forward. It may feel good avoiding it at the time, but the reward won't be as satisfying in the end. In this case, the discomfort we may have felt was nothing compared to the discomfort to those who went through the events of 9/11.

Takeaway: It's important to do things we don't like to do sometimes. Life is not perfect, nor will it ever be.

Rock Stars

#23 - Mount Monroe / #24 - Mount Washington

9/22/2016

Nothing is impossible; the word itself says, "I'm possible!" —Audrey Hepburn

Some hikes are better than others. Some are easy, some have great conditions, some come together organically, and some just hit the right spot at the right moment. This was one of those hikes, with all of the above elements and one of those that simply hit the spot. The hike up Washington and Monroe marked several important milestones for me. It was a big one in so many ways. The weather conditions couldn't have been better, sunny and warm but not hot. It was also a weekday into later September, so there were very little crowds compared to the busy summer season, for the most part.

I hiked with Chris again. I always enjoyed his great attitude and sense of humor. It made for a pleasant day and motivated the hell out of me. As with many periods of this forty-eight journey, I took a bit of a break, then seemed to go into a flurry of hiking again.

Mt. Washington is a bit of an anomaly among White Mountains four-thousand-footers. It's the only 4k with a road. It also has a cog railway. Both methods of transportation afford the ability for anyone to enjoy the highest peak in the Northeast with the worst weather in the world. So, it's usually a zoo up there in the busy summer season. Hordes of people.

Chris and I wandered our way up Ammonoosuc Ravine trail past an AMC hut, up to Mt. Monroe. This was one of the few times we had a summit all to ourselves. The air was fresh and the skies were partly cloudy, which was great for watching shadows of the clouds drift by on the landscape in front of us. One of the reasons we had the summit to ourselves is because the Lakes of the clouds hut had just closed. Often referred to as the "lakes of the crowds", it's the one that serves the folks who go on the make the trek to Mt. Washington, and Mt. Monroe is an even shorter, more convenient walk away from it.

For most of these hikes as you bump into fellow hikers, the conversation differs quite a bit. Many of the folks up there are pretty serious about their hiking. It's not uncommon for me to scrape my way up to a peak and talk to someone who "has a cold, a broken leg, and three hernias, but could only do four peaks today." Most conversations revolve around how quickly they climb, or how many peaks they've done, either in the past or on their current trip. I may be exaggerating slightly, but you get the point.

I've learned a long time ago that I hike my hike, as slow and methodical as that hike may be. BUT I can still get dejected hearing all the stories of glory from everyone else about the accomplishments of doing a presi-traverse.

A presi-traverse is a one-day hike of the entire Presidential Range: seven peaks over a distance of about 23 miles, with close to 9,000 feet of total elevation gain. I got to hear people who were doing the grid, which is all forty-eight peaks done in each month. In other words, Mt. Washington done in January, February, March, etc. for all twelve months. Now replace Mt. Washington with all of the other forty-seven peaks until complete. That's the grid. Brutal.

With all of the potential discouragement from other hikers on other peaks, Mt. Washington turned out to be a pleasant surprise for both of us. We were treated like rock stars. Some folks simply couldn't believe we would climb such a thing. People who had driven up or taken the cog simply couldn't believe that was actually possible. "You hiked up? Really? How long did that take you?" A couple even wanted their photo with us. We embarrassingly obliged, backpacks still on.

We walked down the connector towards Jewell trail. It follows the cog railway tracks for a bit. The cog was making its way up with a fresh batch of tourists, and they were waving at us like we were heroes. They were all taking photos as if we were hiking

Everest, or the circumference of the world or something. Neither Chris nor I ate any of that up at all, as both of us are fairly shy, but it was fun nonetheless.

As noted before, this hike broke several milestones for me. One was the halfway point. I only had twenty-four to go. These hikes were getting easier and easier, and the finish line didn't seem so far away after all. Another was, well, Washington. It's the big boy. Everything goes downhill from here. At an elevation of 6,288 feet, there's simply nothing taller for the forty-eights, or in the Northeast for that matter.

The last milestone was my comfort zone. As with so many of these hikes, I get nervous when everyone talks about the difficulty of the trails there and back. Thoughts of *Is this too tough?* or *Will I be able to do this?* dance in my head. The truth was, and I'm not saying this to sound conceited in any way, that the trails were challenging, but far from impossible. No big deal, really. I remember thinking *That's it? I was freaked out over that?*. In the grand scheme of things, the same goes for life. We wind up this big production in our heads. We cause worry and resistance, but when the goal is accomplished, we often think *That's it? That was challenging but far easier than I thought.*

Takeaway: Are you overthinking anything that may be a smaller challenge than you're making it out to be? Is it worth tackling one of the biggest or hardest parts of a goal early to prove the rest may not be nearly as bad as you thought?

Bring Your Ski Pants

#25 - Mount Liberty

2/14/2017

"Just play. Have fun. Enjoy the game." -Michael Jordan

Now over the halfway mark, and the wind at my back, I was newly energized for the completion. Chris joined me yet again and we picked another beautiful day for this one. February in the White Mountains can be brutal, and it can also be deadly. There are a select few days that it can be gentle and calm. We cherry-picked a wonderful, warm, and calm February day to do this one. I'm glad we did.

As with past hikes, having the company of a friend to share both the challenge and the victory of completion made a big difference.

Liberty is one I had done several times in the past; it's the next-door neighbor to Flume on one side, and Lincoln to the other. Its easy grade in the beginning was perfect for warming us up in preparation for the real climb. Mt. Liberty is far from the hardest mountain in the White Mountain National Forest, but the last half of it is challenging.

With the prospect of hiking a four-thousand-footer

in the middle of winter, I managed to probably scare Chris half to death, by asking him to bring much more than he normally would for a standard hike. This was his first winter hike on a 4k. We brought snowshoes, crampons, extra layers, and snow pants. Chris understood the need for most but questioned the snow pants. "Bring them," I said. "Trust me." Trust me he did, and with fully stuffed backpacks we muscled our way up Liberty.

The snow was well packed and frozen, so we weren't going to posthole at all. With the need for snowshoes being unnecessary, they basically turned into giant weights hanging off the backs of our packs. Always better to bring them just in case, though. I guess we could have worn them going up the trail, but picture an already difficult climb, and then add several pounds, and size fifty shoes on your feet. Snowshoeing can be great fun, but it also can be an enormous amount of work, especially if you have the honor of breaking trail after a snowfall, sometimes measured in several feet.

With what felt like pianos on our backs, we made our way up that well-packed trail to the summit. Beautiful views, light winds, and the warm sun made for a welcomed visit. I love winter hiking for a variety of reasons. First, I love the cold. I'm a rarity in that regard, but I love the winter. People who haven't winter hiked probably don't know the amount of heat generated during a strenuous hike in the cold. Although we were well prepared with several layers, a light jacket did the trick on the way up. We bundled up a bit more on the summit with our sweat quickly evaporating in the breeze, and rapidly cooling us off.

The other reason I love winter hiking is that there are no rocks. That's another thing people who haven't winter hiked don't realize. The snowpack covers the boulders, so walking is much easier. With winter spikes or crampons (which are a form of larger spikes) on, you can easily tackle snow and most ice situations you may encounter.

The summit was open, with a 360-degree view, and it was beautiful. We settled down and had a bite to eat and a beer, chatting with a few folks who were also on their forty-eight quest as well.

As we started to descend, we slowly shuffled down the steep part that approached the summit. We then came to a slightly smoother, flatter part of the trail. I stopped and started to rummage through my pack and told Chris, "Put your snow pants on; this is why we brought them." Confused but unquestioning, Chris pulled them out and put them on.

I proceeded to sit down, right on the packed trail, and said, "You probably thought I was crazy, but now you'll thank me," and with a small push with my hands on the trail, I started sledding down the hill on my behind. This is affectionately known in the hiking world as butt-sledding. After nearly removing our manhood from stumps or trees mid-trail a few times, we decided that may be enough, but just the same, it was worth a few laughs and certainly offered me the feeling of being a kid again, even just for a little while. Chris had much better balance than me, so he removed his spikes, and slid "surfer" style down quite a bit more with just his boots.

Since the beginning of this venture, I've learned a great deal. I've learned so much in general from hiking, actually. One of the biggest is the act of self-discipline, and having the correct mindset of forward, onward, and upward. Simply put, keep moving forward, and keep climbing. Another very important lesson on this hike was that it's okay to have fun and to slide once and awhile. It's allowed.

Takeaway: Stay focused and disciplined, but give yourself permission to have fun in that process.

That's it?

#26 - Mt. Jackson

5/29/2017

"Protect your enthusiasm from the negativity of others." -H. Jackson Brown, Jr.

As with several climbs before this (when will I learn?), I misled myself into thinking this would be a far harder hike than it really was. I heard warnings of how tough and steep it was. I was given warnings about the slide near the end and I exaggerated them in my head. Of course, when you read letters to the editor in the New Hampshire Union Leader like this, what more could you think?

"To the Editor: My husband and I were hiking the Mount Jackson trail on May 27 with my son and family. We are veteran backpackers with 40 years of hiking experience. The trails in the White Mountains are a disgrace.

You have to negotiate boulders and, basically, hike rocky stream beds to gain the most meager vistas and distance. These trails are dangerous and limit safe use to only athletes. All hiking trails anywhere have potential hazards for the unprepared. But the Mount Jackson trail raises those hazards to unacceptable levels. The boulders should be reduced to proper steps and the last section should have hand holds for safety. Trail maintenance should be a state priority so that more residents of New Hampshire can enjoy the beautiful mountains without risking serious injury." - Letter to the editor - Union Leader, June 8, 2017

I know my fellow hikers and I got an enormous kick out of this one. It was written by a woman from Alabama, who, apparently was up here on vacation. She also, in forty years of hiking, must not have done many difficult climbs. Boulders reduced to proper steps? Too funny.

All kidding aside, it's the people like that who raise caution and unnecessary fear, often preventing people like me from extending my boundaries. Actually, I make it sound like it's her fault, but truthfully, the blame is all mine for listening to and believing people like that to begin with.

Negative or alarmist people in our lives have a way of exacerbating fear. They feed off the sensationalism it brings, and obtain a sort of rush or high from making things sound worse than they really are, just as a drug might do.

Like mountains before, this one took a bit of relentless convincing to myself to get up, but I did it. That seems to be a new theme to me in my life, and I'm not complaining. Early on with these hikes, I could have very well have named this book "I didn't want to do it, but I still did it."

Mt. Jackson is the southernmost peak in the Presidential Range and at an elevation of 4,052 feet, it's also the shortest. With a lot of these four-thousand footers, don't let the height fool you. I've been asked many times, "What's an easy 4k that you recommend I can do?" my answer is always the same. There are no easy four-thousand footers. Some are easier than others, but none are easy.

The views on Jackson were gorgeous, and it was one of the few times I took my pack off at the summit, propped it behind my head like a pillow and laid down, just to watch the clouds go by. I think my relaxed state came from a combination of the weather, the warm sun on my face, and the relief of knowing the hike wasn't as bad as I thought it was going to be. Easy? No. An impossible hike with impassable and dangerous boulders and obstacles? Oh, God no.

I decided this was the last hike I was going to either listen to, or believe the gloom and doom reports about. I would always respect the opinions of others regarding trails and trail conditions, but I made an oath to go into them open-minded at this point. No more sleepless nights, and no more hiking day jitters. If they were hard, then I would judge that for myself as I did them.

Takeaway: Are you being fed by a negative source in your life? The six o'clock news? A friend or a loved one addicted to the manifestation of fear in other people's lives? Take notice and gentle action if you are. Turn off the television, or tune out the negativity.

Inspiration in the Right Places

#27 - Mt. Whiteface / #28 - Mt. Passaconaway

6/4/2017

"Life opens up opportunities to you, and you either take them or you stay afraid of taking them." -Jim Carrey

With the help and encouragement of a friend, I banged out two more. This is another hike that had a frightening part to it. Blueberry Ledge. The guidebook states as being "one of the most difficult in the Whites." After my oath on the previous hike, I wasn't very intimidated by this one, though, and I think there are two reasons behind that.

1. I had been on some tough hikes that didn't seem so difficult after I finished them, and I had gained far more confidence in my hiking ability. And after hearing so many scary stories or trail reports that didn't hold water, I wasn't buying it this time. Cautious? Yes. Scared? No.

2. My friend on the other hand was a little nervous, so I went into "we can do this, no problem" mode to help her, much like so many people had done for me before. By taking my mind off myself, I was able to

lead, versus follow.

My friend had done forty-something of the 4k's up to this point, and if she could keep doing these, scared or not, I knew damn well I could too. She is, like so many I know or have helped me hike, a huge role model and inspiration to me. I had suggested as we were headed up, that if we needed to turn back, I was cool with that. I can assure you that she let me know there was no way in hell that was going to happen. Scared or not, that mountain was getting hiked. Case closed.

Among so many other inspirations to me was a man who stood out, named Randy Pierce. Randy did all forty-eight in one single winter season a few years back. That should be inspiration enough, but the fact that he's blind is simply mind-blowing. Randy wasn't born blind but lost his sight due to a neurological disorder in his thirties. I've had the pleasure of meeting him a few times and picking his brain a bit, as I greatly admire inspirational people. His tenacity and resilience has helped me in not only overcoming my own shortcomings or obstacles, but he has also helped me to stop making excuses why I can't do something, and to start concentrating on the reasons I should and can.

Randy not only has done the forty-eight peaks several times but he's also participated in marathons, Tough Mudders, and has climbed Mt. Kilimanjaro in Africa.

After going through two major depressions, I found that I needed to do the work in order to help myself get better. Part of doing that work was looking for people who were able to overcome the odds against them and shine. My friend Randy was one, and my friend on this hike was another.

I had an epiphany after my last hike on Mt. Jackson, and I brought that knowledge to this hike.

Being scared and excited are the same thing.

They are the same physical reactions to an outside stimulus. Your heart beats faster, the adrenaline pumps a little harder, and your breathing becomes a bit shallower. Now, every time I'm scared, I tell myself I'm excited. There's a lot of power and truth in those statements.

Twenty peaks remained, and I had about six months left to do them. I wasn't scared, though; I was excited.

Takeaway: The next time you're scared, remind yourself that it's the same thing as being excited.

Let it Slide

#29 - Middle Tripyramid / #30 - North Tripyramid

6/8/2017

"The journey of a thousand miles begins with one step." -Lao Tzu

I had hiked five peaks in just over two weeks. I was pleased and really started believing that I was going to get these done in time. I only had eighteen left after today's pair, and many of them were multiple peak trips as well.

The Tripyramids were notorious for their slides. Slides are sort of just how they sound. They're generally flat slabs of rock you need to climb up (or down). They can range anywhere from a few feet to a mile or more in length. Slides are often caused by a landslide, as there isn't enough depth to the topsoil to keep the vegetation well rooted on the slab. Slides are naturally being created on a regular basis in the White Mountains. The slides up the Tripyramids are older, and the most popular trails up to the summits.

There are two slides on either end of the ridge. North Slide and South. Most folks make their way up the much steeper North slide, and carefully make their way down the South. Slides can be difficult to descend, especially if they're wet. Remember my earlier mention of wet rocks being as slippery as ice? Picture yourself coming down a giant slab of it. At least with ice, you can wear some sort of spikes to catch into the ice; there's really nothing you can do with wet rock, except pray. We opted to do things a bit different, and take the South slide up, and Scaur's ridge trail down. We avoided the north slide that way, and the ridge trail down, although rarely used, was spectacular. Because of the very nature of where the trails are placed, you often don't get to see what you just climbed. Because Scaur's ridge looped to the side of the three peaks as it descended, it afforded a beautiful view of the ridge we had just climbed. My other thought process behind the trail selections was that I just wanted to get the peaks done. I didn't need bragging rights to the hardest hikes or trails I could do. With newfound hiking confidence, that day will come though.

The South Slide was a blast. With my new "fear is just excitement in disguise" attitude, I went into this one, with the help of a good friend, excited. The South Slide was challenging. Not only was it a steep slide, but it was also full of scree. Scree is either gravel, or small stones on the trail. Walking on scree, especially descending, can sometimes be the equivalent of walking on millions of marbles. You can often lose your footing on it, with small stones tumbling down behind you, as it's tough to know where to step, and the gravel can give way at any point.

Similar to many other ridge-like hikes, when we reached the ridgeline, it was a welcome sight. The trail flattened, and we happily hopped over the three summits. The Tripyramids are aptly named for the three conical shaped peaks that make up the ridge as part of the Sandwich Range. Only two of them officially count as a 4k though, as the prominence of one of the peaks isn't quite enough to qualify it.

It's been a repeated theme throughout this journey, but you know, life is really just about putting one foot in front of the other. Eventually, we all get to where we need to be. One small step at a time. Sometimes we get lost and need to retrace our steps to find the path. Sometimes we just need to bushwhack through the shrubs and undergrowth, sometimes it's all uphill, and other times it's just a casual stroll. Most times, the walk is never quite as bad as we had envisioned it would be. though. One step at a time. Forward, onward, and upward. Little by little.

Takeaway: Life is meant to be lived forward, always forward. Bad day? Leave it behind you for a better day tomorrow, a better afternoon in front of you, or a better next minute. Don't live your life in the future, but keep the hope that you have the power to change that future.

Slow Down

#31 - Carter Dome

6/26/2017

"Just take your time - wave comes. Let the other guys go, catch another one." -Duke Kahanamoku

Carter Dome was a solo trip this time around. This was a rugged and steep one for sure. My legs were aching a bit after climbing the summit. I had a lot on my mind at this point, but I had certainly caught the hiking bug again. For the first time, I had a series of goals lined up for myself, and this one was taking me by storm. I had to admit, I was liking most it.

The long drives, the extended hikes up the hills, and the seemingly even longer trips back home sometime equaled fourteen to sixteen-hour days. Most of it I enjoyed. Some of it I didn't. But that's an important aspect of life. It isn't always going to be all roses. There are parts that suck. There's nothing you'll enjoy doing all the time. Some things are hard, and they are what they are. But those are the things that make you great and separate you from everyone else. THOSE are the defining moments in your life that make the rest of it seem that much easier. The sucky parts are what help to make you great, and the sucky parts are what make the good parts seem that much better.

As with many of these hikes, especially in better weather, I wanted to get up to the trailhead, push through the hike, and just get back down. I wanted to come back to a fresh change of socks, a beer, and drive home as quickly as possible. With this "must get up, must get down" mantra playing in my head, I got to it right away. I took the 19-mile brook trail to start. It's a beautiful, 1.9-mile, relatively flat trail that follows along the 19-mile brook itself. It's a free-flowing river that parallels the trail for much of the distance. Running water, like streams or rivers, are as good company as I've had on any hike. I guess with the sound of babbling water, you don't feel so alone.

With my head down and determination in my soul, I shifted into fifth gear and started trucking up the trail. My mind was working overtime. *I should be at the summit for 12:00. If I stay for about 15 minutes and turn around, then I should be off summit and back on 19-mile brook by 1:00. From there I should be back to the trailhead by 3:00. Beer and food by 4:00, home by 8:00. What's my elevation? Cool still on pace...* And so on, and so on...

About a mile into the trail, I quickly caught up to a man and a young boy steadily walking ahead of me. The boy was maybe only eleven or twelve years old. They both had common backpacks. By that, I mean the kind you may use for books at school, or you might buy at a department store. The boy's walking stick was a simple straight branch he had found along the trail. As I approached from behind, still in *gotta get this done* mode, I gave a quick hello.

The boy smiled and spoke very politely with a heavy accent. "Hello, sir, how are you today?" We all stopped on the trail, and I told him I was well. We asked where each was going, as this trail had several options to hike toward. The man answered, "We're headed to the Carter Notch hut to spend the night, maybe do Mt. Hight tomorrow." I explained my plans of Carter Dome, tried to wrap up the conversation politely, and turned to go when the boy asked, "Would you join us walking for a little while?" I was surprised at the request, but said I would indeed join them on their walk for a bit.

As we slowly and methodically walked, the boy spoke at length about his upbringing in the Ukraine. He explained that his grandfather had raised enough money to send him to the United States for a long summer visit, and the man was a family friend he was staying with. He told me about his life there, and asked me countless questions about life here in America. His questions were both thoughtful and thought-provoking. I guess I had never taken the time to think about what living here means to me, or how we live life in general. More than anything else, that young boy taught me to slow down.

Our conversation was supposed to be enriching for him, but I can assure you was more so for me. He taught me far more than I taught him.

After extended conversation and grateful goodbyes for time spent together, I headed off again. I was very blessed as I continued to bump into several AT through hikers making their way closer to Maine. Taking a lesson from my earlier conversation with the man and boy, I took extra time to ask them all about their journey so far, their reasons for doing the Appalachian Trail, favorite moments, and what they had learned up to this point. It was fascinating to hear their answers, and, again, I was grateful that the boy had taken the time to get to know me a little earlier, so I could pass that along to enrich my life even more, and encourage someone else's.

Takeaway: Are you taking the time to slow down enough to listen to others and find out what makes them tick, what their hopes and dreams are, and what plans they may have for the future?

Take Action

#32 - Mt. Adams / #33 - Mt. Madison

7/2/2017

"When you get to the top, keep climbing."

—*Zen proverb*

With the help and encouragement of two friends, and only one week after completing Carter Dome, with my legs still feeling it, I joyfully climbed one of the hardest set of peaks in the White Mountains. Mt. Adams and Mt. Madison. Rocky, difficult, and over five thousand feet of total elevation gain. These are both part of the Presidential Range, and I felt like I simply ate them up. I also woke up the next day feeling more alive and refreshed than ever. I had been killing the 4k's and hiking locally every day. It had been energizing and a purposeful habit for sure, one I could use at that point.

We ran into many kind hikers that day, one who had undertaken this hike as her first in the White Mountains. A daunting feat indeed! You meet lots of people on the trails: the new and unprepared, the older and overprepared, the uninformed (much like I was on my first summit so many years ago), and the experienced, willing to share their knowledge with the world about what they've learned hiking.

With another hut conveniently placed on this one, we had that opportunity to meet so many of those people. We climbed Airline trail, a popular path that leads up to the Northernmost peaks in the Presidential Range.

As we neared the summit, the pile of boulders to maneuver reminded me of a beach jetty. Large stones, about the size of Volkswagens were strewn everywhere, in seemingly random fashion. One false step or slip, and you could easily break a leg in the cracks and crevices between them. Although my fear of hiking the difficult hikes has subsided considerably, I still have enormous respect for the difficult parts of these mountains, and still needed to be reminded of the dangerous nature of these climbs sometimes.

The weather is an unpredictable thing in the White Mountains. Even on this day, in July, we stood at the summit in layers, winter hat, and gloves. When you factor in the wind evaporating the sweat from the hard climb up, lack of warm sun due to clouds, and a significant drop in temperature, hypothermia is a very real possibility, even in July.

As we came off of Adams, toward the hut and Mt. Madison, we rounded the corner to Star Lake and I was reminded of a young lady who died in that very spot, the previous winter. It was a brutally cold and windy day. She was a very skilled and experienced mountaineer. So, she took the chance on a hike that day and paid the ultimate price. The weather forecasts can only be so accurate, and the weather will always do what it pleases. The difference between ten degrees and twenty miles per hour on the wind speeds can literally mean the difference between life and death on some occasions, especially up here.

We were wise enough to do Mt. Adams first, as getting up Mt. Madison wasn't bad, but would have been tougher if we had reversed the order of the peaks.

The descent was uneventful in a good way. The conversation was engaging as we went down Valley way, an easy footed, gradual trail that felt good on the legs after a wonderfully challenging climb.

And just like that, they were done. Two of the hardest summits in the Northeast.

Takeaway: Life, much like the mountains, need to be both experienced and respected fully.

Mountain Karma

#34 - Mt. Cabot

7/9/2017

"There is wisdom in climbing mountains, for they teach us how truly small we are." -Jeff Wheeler

"Knock knock..."

"Who's there?"

"Humility."

"Who?"

"Humility."

"Where did you come from? You just popped up from out of the blue. What do you want?"

"Nothing much, I just want to knock you down a few pegs before you get too full of yourself."

Mt. Cabot is the Northernmost summit of the four-thousand-footers, just shy of ninety minutes from the Canadian border. The day started perfectly with an eagle sighting at the trailhead. I got a few decent photos of it and then just watched it proudly glide across the sky for a while. Peacefully and quietly he soared, just letting the thermal winds take him to where he wanted to go. Wings outstretched, and effortless. The eagle knew what he was doing, and had much respect for the wind. I, on the other hand, lost respect for these mountains, if only for a day.

After completing the difficult Adams and Madison, without issue, I decided to tackle Cabot. I almost gloated about Adams and Madison not being a big deal, since they're two of the hardest peaks you can climb. They were both supposedly brutal, yet they didn't turn out to be too bad, surprisingly.

Cabot, on the other hand, is supposed to be one of the easiest one can do with decent footing and an elevation of just over four thousand feet. It's a long ride to get to, but listed as a moderate, easier climb.

This is another one of those peaks people recommend to others for their first four-thousand-footer. With all this talk and chatter about how easy it supposedly was in my head, I figured I would skip all the way up without a whimper and prance all the way back down, barely breaking a sweat.

Then humility paid me a visit (see interaction above). This mountain kicked my ass. I simply wasn't mentally ready or prepared for it. I did it, but not without some disappointment in myself, and perhaps some creative cussing. I was reminded of a few very important things by this mountain.

1. Most hiking is mental, not physical.

2. ALL the 4k's are hard. That's why people hike

them. There are no easy ones. Easier than others, yes. Just plain easy? No.

3. Never get too full of yourself. You will take the fall. That's the way the universe works. You push; it pushes back. You flow; it flows. You respect it; it respects back.

A good lesson learned, and a promise to myself to never take any of these mountains or their difficulties for granted, because if I do, I'll get my ass handed to me on a platter again.

With perfect weather and a chance to finally see the infamous, almost abandoned cabin near the summit, there were some good highlights to the hike, as there are in all of them. Another pleasant surprise came in the form of seeing some folks who were also attempting their forty-eight I had met on the Madison and Adams hike just the week before. Totally random, and another testament to the community nature of the hikers up there. We met in disbelief and had a few laughs over the chance encounter.

For as tough as any of these hikes were, there was always something I could be grateful for. I was most grateful for the lesson in respecting the mountains that this peak taught me.

Takeaway: Never get too full of yourself. You will take the fall. That's the way the universe works. You push; it pushes back. You flow; it flows. You respect; it respects back.

Honor the Struggle

#35 - Mt. Moriah

7/24/2017

"Stay Centered, honor the struggle, know you can handle this" —Brendon Burchard

The week before this, I had driven all the way up to the Moriah trailhead and decided to call off the hike. I sat in my car arguing with myself for almost thirty minutes before I concluded to skip it. I was exhausted. It's always important to push yourself, especially when you don't feel like doing something you need to do, but some days, especially with in hiking, you either have it that day, or you don't. That day, I didn't.

After a false start the week before, I got my butt out of bed, crawled into the car, and hauled myself three and a half hours up to the Carter range to attempt hiking Mt. Moriah, again.

Have you ever come to a point during the completion of a goal, when you thought "What's the use?" or "Why on earth am I doing this?"

No? You haven't either? I didn't think so.

So why did I keep going? Because I knew that I

would appreciate later what I was working hard at on any given day. During a bout with major depression, I kept telling myself that depression itself would be the best thing that ever happened to me. Did I feel like it during that depression? No. After going through the depression, did I feel like it was the best thing that ever happened to me? Undoubtedly.

So far, the biggest goal I had ever achieved was getting myself through that depression. I say getting myself through, because that's exactly what I did. I worked on the things that needed to be done to bring me to a final outcome. In this case, managing the depression, and just feeling well. I read the books, I talked it out, I watched the videos, I did the physical exercise, and I reprogrammed my brain to stop being its own worst enemy. I learned about how my brain worked, what caused depression, and what worked to help curb it; then, I did it. I knew that if I kept going forward, I would get there. I was beginning to realize that goals and challenges don't always have to be physical things. Most goal attainment has a mental aspect. Without the correct mentality, we're far less likely to persist and eventually conquer not only our goals but also ourselves.

Mt. Moriah was a pretty mountain. I had done some of the Carter Range at that point, so the views were familiar, although no less spectacular. In order to summit the peak, you need to climb over Mt.

Surprise mid-way through the hike. Apparently, it's very aptly named, because I had no idea I had gone over it!

Not thinking I had reached the summit of Mt. Surprise yet, I thought I was much father back in the hike than I planned. With continued good vibes, I pressed on, waiting for this Mt. Surprise to show itself. Just before I reached the summit of Moriah, I realized where I actually was in the hike, and a feeling of elation came over me. What I thought was a few miles left to go, turned out to be about a half mile. A few fellow hikers I had met along the way fell for the same trap. Descending the mountain, we saw what Mt. Surprise is, a small, open bump along the way. Hardly something to call a separate mountain, but worth a few laughs and a memorable story, anyway.

Just as with getting through my depression, I continue to look at challenges as lessons to be taught and temporary burdens to be enlightened from.

So, I kept getting up early and hiked the big mountains, one after the other. They were hard, and were are many I did not feel like doing.

After they are all done, I knew it would be one of the best things that ever happened to me.

Takeaway: Honor the struggle. Most are the best things that will ever happen to you.

Nice Kitties

#36 - Wildcat A / #37 - Wildcat D

8/1/2017

"If we don't change direction soon, we'll end up where we're going." -Irwin Corey

When is the last time you've taken care of yourself? This subject comes up because some of the parts of this goal had really helped me to gain confidence, self-discipline, and an overall better understanding of my physical limits. I've forced myself to get up early, driven three to four hours, hiked sometimes ten to twelve miles, then driven back home the three to four hours again.

I had planned to hike Owl's head, an eighteen-mile slog, and recognized that on this day, my time was better off sleeping a little later, spending time with family, and reassessing some things that needed it. I knew I would hike it another day. There's a fine line for walking away from our goals too easily, and accomplishing what needs to be accomplished. If we listen carefully though, we can usually separate the two and come up with a logical reasoning that works toward accomplish our goals, yet still allows us to properly take care of ourselves. I believe that this is the best thing for us in the long run.

With time taken the day before to mentally and physically recuperate, I decided to hike Wildcat A. It's a fairly steep but sort of uneventful peak. My original plans as this goal progressed were to finish my forty-eighth peak on Wildcat D, its nearby cousin, not too far away along the ridge. Wildcat D is also a ski area, so my thinking was that if anyone wanted to join me, they could always take a gondola ride up to the summit. For my benefit, I could walk down the easy ski area trail after summiting (rules state that you must go up and down the mountains unassisted by anything manmade).

Long story short, I not only hiked Wildcat A without issue, but it felt so good, I pressed on to do Wildcats B, C, and D as well. Making a grand loop, and walking down the ski slope, then three miles up busy route 16 back to my car at Nineteen Mile Brook, where I originally parked. There's a Wildcat E as well, but only A and D count towards the 4k list, so I didn't feel the need to press on to the last one. It felt *so* good to push myself a bit, and try something a little unplanned. Sometimes, those calculated risks we take in life can be so fulfilling!

One unusual moment in the hike was my decision to take that ski trail down Wildcat D to Route 16, the route I had originally intended to be as my last. The ski area allows this on one of their trails in the offseason, named Polecat. This trail brought up an unusual quandary. How would you label or consider what a difficult trail is? I say this, because when people have asked me what the hardest trail on the whole journey was, I often include this ski trail.

Polecat was basically just an average, easy access road sidewinding up and down the mountain. The problem was that it was also the only trail I fell multiple times on, and drew blood on numerous occasions. I think the combination of gravity, a clear path, and the rocky scree kept my feet from stabilizing. Was it a hard trail? No, I guess. It was just a gravel road. Was it difficult to come down? Very, actually.

With bloodied knees and elbows, and a good laugh over the unexpected difficulty of the trail, I finally made it down safely. I walked the long walk along Route 16, past the Mt. Washington Auto road, and back to the 19-mile brook trailhead.

If I hadn't decided to take care of myself earlier by not hiking Owl's head, I would have never experienced this one in the way that I did. As for the last peak I wanted to finish on now? I didn't know. I was thinking Bondcliff, maybe.

Takeaway: Learn to reassess and regroup in your goals and in your life. Things can be done more than just one way, and you can often change or adjust the rules accordingly for it as well, if needed.

Hello, Old Friends

#38 - Mt. Lincoln / #39 - Mt Lafayette

8/9/2017

"You collect people to take with you. Some people change, other people don't... it's wonderful because I've met some incredible friends." -Imogen Poots

Over thirty years ago I hiked my first four-thousand-footers, Mt. Lincoln and Mt. Lafayette. Those were the ones (like for so many other people) that hooked me into climbing a multitude of mountains, including the forty-eight four-thousand footers since then. After my first harrowing trip up them, hiking now involves the elements of both controlled risk and danger that remind you that you're not only alive but that a hard, physical day are welcomed friends when it's all said and done.

I had done this loop a total of five times already, this being my sixth, but hadn't hiked them in over fifteen years. In some ways, it was like seeing an old familiar friend again. Have you ever gotten together with an old acquaintance, and you found they hadn't changed that much, but you had changed to the point where the relationship wasn't quite the same as before? These peaks felt very much like that. It almost felt like a hike I had never done before, because my views about hiking and my capabilities had changed, not the mountains themselves.

As I was coming near the end of completing the forty-eight, it also felt like a sort of coming full circle, hiking the two peaks that got me started four-thousand-footers to begin with. To top off the whole hike, I took someone who had never hiked a 4k before, so it was great to see the beauty of this special hike through his eyes as if it were my first time hiking them as well.

The Lincoln-Lafayette loop, as I mentioned in the introduction, has been named one of the best hikes in the United States, and in some cases, the world by some pretty popular publications. On one hand, I'm so fortunate to have these so close to home and accessible almost any time I'd like. On the other hand, their newfound popularity has made it a virtual zoo, especially on the weekends. During the summer months, on popular Saturdays and Sundays, the large parking lots fill to overflowing and the cars park for what seem like miles along busy Route 3 in Franconia Notch just to climb this famous loop.

We opted for a cloudy and cool weekday, which kept the crowds at bay. I can now see why this is considered one of the best hikes in the country. Waterfalls, an almost knife-edge ridge, stunning views, easy accessibility off the highway, three peaks (two of which count toward the 4k list), part of the

Appalachian trail, a hut, and a nine-mile hike that's challenging, but won't kill you. What's not to love about it?

I've mentioned this before, but when it's a slightly overcast day, there's nothing more magical than to watch the shadows of the clouds drift by across the mountains in the distance. It almost gives a sense of perspective to just how large and majestic these mountains really are. It also gives perspective as to what you've climbed, gaining the ability to watch cloud shadows drift by on distant mountains, looking so small against the mighty hills.

Along with another former farm store employee, Chris joined us as well. These were Chris's first big mountains climbed on a previous outing with friends a few years before, and he couldn't wait to see them again, too.

We arrived early to a nearly empty parking lot. The climb was slow and methodical for me, the younger guys patiently put up with my speed. We had a lot of fun, though. I don't spend much time on the summits, but we took the time on the final peak, Lafayette, to hunker down for a bite and enjoy the views; then, at the hut, we warmed up a bit and sat out of the wind.

It was nice to introduce these mountains to someone new. I think I've taken maybe a dozen folks up this ridge and these mountains for their first real hiking excursion at one time or another. It's always been a tried and true go to hike when I was asked to introduce someone to the four-thousand-footers of the White Mountains.

I said hello to my old friends, Lincoln and Lafayette. We had a good laugh over my first climb across them, and I said goodbye until next time. These are old friends I know I'll see again soon. They aged well, and were more beautiful than ever. More beautiful than I remember them to be, truth be told.

Takeaway: Have you ever taken the time to see things with new eyes, as if for the first time? Have you ever been able to experience something for the first time again through someone else's experience?

What Else Would I Rather be Doing?

#40 - Mt. Isolation

8/20/2107

"It's not raining - it's sunny - we are happy, we are in good company & we are alive -What else would we rather be doing?" —Amy Dalrymple

I know that I've mentioned attitude many times. I simply cannot stress enough that in order to meet a challenge, you need to be mentally prepared to face that challenge, take each obstacle head on, and most importantly, *believe* you can do it. What seems impossible to us starts to become more realistically possible as we continue to push through whatever we need to push through, and move past whatever scares or tires us.

It's okay to be scared, but it's not okay to avoid life because you're scared. Sometimes, we need to do things terrified and accomplish things with our knees knocking, teeth chattering, and afraid. I'm not talking about anything life-threatening, but fear of the common things that hold us back, like *What will other people think about me?* or *I don't want to do that because I'll look foolish.* Just as we can also talk ourselves into facing a challenge, it's very easy to talk ourselves out of one as well.

This hike was all about a positive attitude, one of my companions, Amy, said it best as the day's mantra. Throughout the toughest sections, she kept repeating: "It's not raining, it's sunny, we are happy, we are in good company, and we are alive. What else would we rather be doing?"

That mantra carried us all day, it carried me through all of the remaining hikes in the journey, and it still carries me today with every hike I do.

I will say, from a "cool" factor, how impressive is the name Mt. Isolation? It almost sounds like something that JRR Tolkien would write about in *Lord of the Rings* or *The Hobbit*. Although fairly desolate, this mountain isn't quite as remote as the name would lead you to believe. Make no mistake, there's really no easy way to get to it, but it wasn't impossible to get in and out of, and we were far from the only ones out hiking it that day. There were surprisingly quite a few people.

This was a mountain that needed to be climbed up to an elevation of almost five thousand feet, along Glen Boulder trail, which skirts a far side of Mt. Washington, we then had to hike down to summit the peak at just over four-thousand feet. An unusual method of getting to the top of a mountain, but that was what needed to be done in order reach the peak. We needed to climb up in order to go down to the summit peak.

We did a spectacular loop, Glen Boulder then

Isolation trail took us to the summit, then Rocky Branch back to another trailhead, where we had car-spotted. The returning trail was another that was supposed to be one of the muddiest, wettest, and dirtiest trails in New Hampshire. It was very rare that I heard something positive said about this trail. Cue in past experiences, and I knew better than to believe it this time. I was correct. Truthfully, I found it to be very pleasant. It meandered down nicely, affording some casual rock hopping, and pleasant trail scenery. Hiking, or more specifically walking can have a distinct rhythm to it, and this trail was perfect for that. The bounce between rocks, the steady step, step, step, step of the flatter parts, and the breath easing in and out can all be almost set to a metronome. The walking is easy, and the breaths are slow and deep.

It felt extra-long just as we neared the end, but many of these can. I have a running joke, especially when I return on the same trail I went up on.

"How long was the trail to Garfield?"

"We took the Garfield trail up and back. Five miles up, eight miles back."

Of course, attitude has a lot to do with suppressing the "are we ever going to finish this frigging hike?" mentality. But I also figure that after ten or eleven hours on the trail, an "is this ever going to end?" or two is allowed near the finale of the day's trek.

I had a good attitude about the past few hikes, but I was so focused on finishing them, I was also starting to burn myself out. The next hike was supposed to be the dreaded Owl's Head.

Takeaway: When things get tough, what's your mantra? What words do you say repeatedly? What words should you be repeating and concentrating on over and over again?

#40.1 Owl's Head (almost...)

There are some defining moments in your life you can pinpoint the exact time of clarity and reason they happened. I had one of those epiphinal moments coming into this particular hike.

Long before my four-thousand-footer adventures, as a child, my family would frequent the White Mountains for our summer vacations. One key and recurring memory of those trips was visiting Franconia Falls. We would take the long, beautiful walk along the Wilderness Trail following the Pemigewassett River to our destination. It was similar to a long rail trail without the asphalt, and occasional railroad ties still embedded in the earth below us. Franconia Falls was about three miles in, about a six mile walk total, with the return trip included. As kids, we could have sworn it was twenty, but you know how that works. At the end of the flat train trestle, before the river crossing, that was called the Wilderness Trail (It's now called Lincoln Woods), we would take a sharp left to reach the falls, just around the corner.

If you were to continue straight ahead, across a wooden bridge, that's where the real wilderness lay. As a young boy, I could only picture the trail leading to the end of the earth and the certainty of getting lost. People simply didn't go out there unless they were super-daring, ultra-experienced, and mega-confident. I knew I sure as hell wasn't. The only thing harder or more impossible than going beyond the falls trail to that unknown wilderness would be hiking the forty-eight four-thousand-footers. Those would certainly take a lifetime to do...

With some foot-dragging, procrastination, and overall dilly-dallying, I just about had these done. The last few months, I had hiked like a man running out of time on his goal, and, in reality, I kind of was. I had done eighteen peaks in the last three months. Most were enjoyable to a certain extent, but all had parts that were tedious, rushed, and exhausting.

No matter how much you hike, the sometimes eight total hours of driving, and twelve mile slogs up to the summits just eventually catch up with you. The mountains were burning me out, and that was one of my fears in taking a goal like this upon myself. The mountains have always been a place of rejuvenation to me, not of misery.

The good news about a goal like this is how much these hikes have taught me. My confidence level had skyrocketed on the trails. I had found many of the difficult and formerly impossible (in my mind) trails were no big deal. Not always done quickly or perfectly, but all pretty do-able in the grand scheme of things.

I now officially only had three trips left to complete them.

I finally decided to tackle Owl's Head. It's that eighteen-mile hike that follows an unmarked, scree covered slide up to a peak with no views. As with a lot of these hikes, I got up at an ungodly hour to drive the two and a half hours to walk eighteen miles until my legs ached, then drive the two and a half hours back home again, alone.

The Goal... Almost done... Must finish...

In order to get to Owl's Head, you need to head out on the trail I used to frequent as a kid, Lincoln woods (formerly the Wilderness trail), and when you get to the end, where I used to turn left to the falls, you need to cross "that" bridge.

This is where the epiphinal moment kicked in... Instead of dismay, horror, and fear of crossing "that bridge," my exact thoughts were; *Meh. I don't want to do this. Not today.*

There's an old saying that goes "Go big or go home." For almost three years I had gone big. This day, in many ways, I went home.

I casually decided to take a left instead of over the bridge, and head to Franconia Falls, where I had so many fond memories growing up. I lay on the rocks for hours in the warm sun, and just listened to the rush of the river. It was at that moment, where I decided to take that left, when I realized that life is not a destination to keep running to, but a journey to be enjoyed at every moment. This is extremely obvious advice and something I always said I believed in, but now it hit me. In my bones hit me. Why am I rushing through this? Why am I rushing through life in general? SLOW DOWN AND ENJOY THIS.

My thoughts turned to realizing that I had plenty of time to finish my forty-eighth peak by the time I had turned fifty years old. I think having that knowledge was as good as completing them to me at that moment. Then again, who cares? It was my goal and my race anyway. I made the rules, nobody else did.

With that said, I decided to leave Owl's Head, as my last peak, for whenever I wanted to do it this year, next year, or in ten years. No more turning friends away for hikes I wouldn't do because I had another peak to do, or I had already bagged that one. No more killing myself to get these done, and no more slogs to places I don't want to go.

I felt so grateful to the friends who had joined me on the journey and so grateful for the lessons that the goal has taught me up to this point. I continued to lie in the warm sun near the falls and wept for a long time. I was tired and felt a burden had been lifted from my shoulders.

In many ways, I felt like I just had a wonderful meal at a gourmet restaurant, and I was just saving the last bite on my plate. I was delaying my gratification and saving the dessert, if you will, for just a little longer. I had decided to just extend the goal and journey for as many moments as possible. One day I'd finish. Or not. It didn't matter.

The idea of crossing "that bridge" as the last hike appealed to me for so many reasons, the most important being a direct metaphor for facing a major fear, and something I once thought so impossible, and conquering it.

I Don't Stop When I'm Tired, I Stop When I'm Done

#41 - North Twin / #42 - South Twin / #43 - West Bond / #44 - Mt. Bond / #45 – Bondcliff

9/24/2017

If you don't risk anything, you risk even more. — Erica Jong

At this point in the trip, when people asked me how many peaks I had left, I would answer, "I'd rather say I have three trips left." Maybe it was psychological, but three trips sounded a hell of a lot better than eight peaks remaining, in total.

The weather was forecast to be in the low 60's, with a light breeze on the summits. Even temperatures in the 60's were a little warm for my taste, but with daylight getting shorter and good friends willing to tackle this with me, we decided to give it a go.

I had a new outlook on the remaining hikes after my Owl's Head epiphany, and beyond just producing a good attitude, I was going to fully embrace this life-changing experience as a whole. Every minute I had left of it.

A lot of folks do this twenty-mile trek in two days. With my back and shoulders beaten up from all the physical labor I had done at the farm store for so many years, I simply couldn't carry a heavier load.

When you decide to camp overnight on a long hike like that, your pack size and weight increase considerably with sleeping bags, tents, additional food, stoves, and cookware. It all adds up. I knew that by just muscling through the entire long walk with a lighter load in one shot, I would be better off physically the day of the hike, and the next day as well.

The good news is that my mind and attitude were both in "enjoy the ride" mode. The bad news was that the hike was brutally difficult for me. The temperature rose to the mid-70's in the beginning stages of the hike. When I tell you how much I lumbered and strained up this hike, I'm not kidding.

About halfway up North Twin, I looked to my partners and said, "I don't think I can do this."

"You mean the whole twenty miles? That's totally cool; don't worry about it," they replied.

"No, I mean I don't think that I can make it up this first peak," I said, exhausted, and I meant it.

We finally made it to North Twin. It took frequent breaks between short spurts of elevation gain, but we summited. My next small goal was to reach South Twin, which I felt was attainable at that point. The remaining four peaks, which included a peak that didn't count towards the list, Mt. Goyot, were in serious question for me though.

When we finally reached the South Twin peak, there were several things working for us at that point. We had enough water, could physically see what we needed to climb ahead of us in the distance, and our main elevation gain was complete, for the most part. We knew it was all relatively downhill from there.

After a long rest on the summit, I decided that I wanted to go for it. I was physically feeling better, the miles ahead were long, but easier than what we had climbed, and I didn't feel like coming back to do this again. I was here and confident in my ability. If I wasn't confident, I would have turned around, with no regrets. The views were simply breathtaking, the company was welcomed and encouraging, and I had made it this far.

We pressed on. The heat was almost unbearable for me. The summit temperatures were almost eighty degrees with no breeze whatsoever, and the hike is open for almost the entire way. No shade at all. "It's like a desert out here," my buddy commented.

The only other wavering moment I had on the hike was bagging West Bond. You see, the main trail leads over all of the other peaks needed, so as long as you keep walking, you have no choice but to summit all of the others. West Bond, on the other hand, is a half-mile side trail to the summit, making it an additional mile total off that main trail. A half mile in, then a half mile back. With some encouragement about having to come back for it if we didn't do it now, I went. West Bond turned out to be one of my favorite peaks on this whole journey. It was a quiet, peaceful summit that afforded spectacular views of our hike ahead, Bond and Bondcliff. We were also able to experience something you can't do very often in the White Mountains. We were able to sit in pure silence, and visually not see anything artificial. The Bonds, particularly West Bond, are in one of the most remote area in the White Mountains, if not New Hampshire. There's no trace of a road, no sound of a plane or car, no cell signals, and very few other people.

After a needed rest, we moved forward, yet again. The hottest part of the hike, by far, was up to the final summit, Bondcliff. One of the most iconic photo opportunities is just off of the summit here. It's a two-thousand-foot vertical drop on an almost pillar like rock formation. The top of the pillar has about a three-foot, square platform to step on for the photo opportunity. I haven't mentioned it yet, but I'm not real fond of heights, and getting to this photo opportunity required a little hop, to the flat, three-foot top part of that formation that has the two-thousand-foot sheer drop. I hesitated for a moment, then, before I could back down, stepped on that square and proudly, if not terrifyingly, got my photo taken.

I did it scared, but I did it. The photo opportunity,

the hike, all of it. I did five four-thousand-footers, six peaks total, and just over twenty miles of rugged hiking.

The remaining walk out was long, but not as bad as the excruciating drive home was. It was one of the few hikes I did that I couldn't even think of having my mouth watering beer at the end. I was too exhausted.

Takeaway: Is there something you need to do scared? What can you do that may be out of your comfort zone that will help you to grow?

Homestretch

#46 - Middle Carter / #47 - South Carter

10/02/2017

"I'm generally more and more in my comfort zone in the wild." -Tom Felton

There have been times when I knew I was making progress toward the end of my journey, but none as much as this hike. With the epic Twins and Bonds adventure behind me, I was simply unstoppable at this point. This hike was completely uneventful in the hiking sense. The trail was average, the summits were okay, and the views were limited at times and unplentiful. This hike also happened to be the most memorable one though. I had purposefully decided to hike it solo to look back on the past hikes and total journey I had done up to that point.

Reminisce I did. I thought about how far I had come, not only in life but also on this particular goal. How so many years ago it seemed inconceivable. I thought about my previous perspective on the silliness of goals and was both sad and elated. I had wasted so much time stubbornly avoiding so many wonderful opportunities to improve myself, but realized that I had plenty of time left to start initiating new goals in my life regarding so many other things.

I thought about the people who had joined me, helped me, and in the process, improved me. I looked back on all of the miles walked, the mountains climbed, and the memories made. Most of all, I realized how grateful I was. Grateful for the help of others, for the time I had to accomplish these, to the book I was going to write that's in your hands now, and most of all, I was grateful to myself for having gotten out of my own way to achieve this. I was grateful about the past, and I was excited for the future.

I met nobody else on this hike, and the miles went by like a flash. It was almost as if it were meant to be, a simple hike. Effortless, beautiful, reflective, warm, refreshing, and solitary.

Takeaways: What are you grateful for? What are you most excited about in your future?

I'll Cross That Bridge When I Get to it.

#48 - Owl's Head

10/20/2017

"Discipline is the bridge between goals and accomplishment." -Jim Rohn

We got an early start to the day, as we had for most of these. My original thoughts about leaving Owl's Head for whenever I wanted to complete them (and the forty-eight, in general) gave me an unexpected boost in hiking the remaining peaks. Maybe it was the sense of freedom I allowed myself, or the "I'm in charge" feeling it gave me to be in control of my destiny, but whatever it was, it worked. Whatever the reason, I was able to enjoy my remaining peaks leading up to Owl's head completely.

Two months ahead of schedule, I was going to finish my forty-eighth and final mountain.

The day was perfectly cool, but not cold. Fallen leaves gave a wonderful autumn aroma and the shoosh of the leaves underfoot reminded me of when I was a kid playing in the forest. The tricky river crossings could be trouble in most years, but being an unusually dry season so far, they were very manageable. It was a relaxed, casual day. Being a slower hiker, I reminded my two companions that today was not to be a race of any kind. I wanted to enjoy this hike, no matter how long it took.

Unlike many, I've always loved Lincoln woods, the long, seemingly endless trestle trail, so I knew that wouldn't be an issue. I was looking forward to it, truthfully. That trail held a lot of fond memories for me.

This was an out and back hike, that started and ended at Lincoln Woods. I knew as we approached and crossed over "that" bridge that passed the trail to the falls to the left, it wouldn't faze me too much emotionally. Coming back, I had the feeling it would.

I had already crossed over it coming back from the Bonds traverse a couple of hikes before this one. We had done it as a car spot, starting at North Twin, then ending at Lincoln woods. This crossing would take on a much different meaning.

We were chatting away, crossed the bridge, and continued onward. This was going to be a long hike, so the conversation was welcomed. As we continued almost two miles past the bridge, still chatting away, we noticed the Pemigewassett River to our right... It wasn't supposed to be there. We had missed the trail we were supposed to take just over the bridge. This was the first, and only time I may add, I'd missed a trail hiking the entire forty-eight. We took a deep breath, laughed it off, and continued back down the Wilderness trail to hook up with the correct one. As we approached the bridge, there was the trail junction just before it. Plain as day. We managed to turn what should have been an eighteen-mile hike into a twenty-two-mile hike, which also happens to be the longest hike I had ever done in my life to that point. Another first on my last peak. If this were easy, everyone would do it, right?

The walking was effortless, and we were all in good spirits, meeting several wonderful folks along the way. River crossings were fun, skipping carefully from rock to rock. We came upon the slide that's the main trail to the summit by a mercifully placed set of cairns on the trail, indicating where we needed to turn right to start the ascent.

The slide was as described: loose scree and a sharp pitch. After walking at a pace of about three miles per hour throughout, it felt much different walking at a pace of under a mile per hour on the slide. The unexpected views were wonderful from the slide itself, and the frequent breaks to admire them and catch my breath were very welcome.

As we approached the summit, several other perplexed hikers who had been well ahead of us approached and asked where the summit actually was.

"There are two summits, I believe" I replied. "One is an old one and one is new. They determined there was a slightly higher spot a few years ago. There's a cairn there, I saw it on a Facebook post a few days ago."

They had reservations in their look and manner, telling me that there was indeed, no cairn. "I bet you didn't go far enough," I noted. So we all trudged on. No cairn. We trudged further to where we knew there was no obvious path any further. No cairn. We were indeed at the highest point and had passed it.

After much deliberation and the use of some GPS technology, we determined that we had actually reached the summit. No indication, with the exception of an open area and an "OH top" carved into a tree. (We would find out upon our return that someone had in fact, removed the cairn).

I'm a believer that a hike isn't complete until the end when you return back to the trailhead. So, with little fanfare or celebration, somewhat still discouraged from the cairn-less summit situation and added time and mileage trying to find it, we headed carefully down the slide to made our way back.

As the trail flattened and the sun was lowering in the sky, my companions had the instinct to walk just ahead of me. This left me to my thoughts about all the lessons I had learned on this journey, people who had joined me, and the overall satisfaction of getting up all those early mornings, taken all the long drives, and climbed all of those mountains by continually putting one foot in front of the other. Over and over and over again.

People have done the forty-eight quicker, and lots of folks have done all of them dozens of times, but this was my version of climbing Mt. Everest. It was my personal demon that needed to be tamed, and it was my toe-dipping moment into the world of completing a physical major goal. At almost age fifty, I may add.

My emotions weren't as strong as I had thought they would be upon crossing that bridge back to Lincoln Woods, which had held me in fear and wonder so many years ago. Or even back at the car with a celebratory beer.

It was only the next day, out of the blue, when I wept uncontrollably and joyfully.

Good God. I had done it. Finally. I completed my forty-eight.

Conclusion

"The world ain't all sunshine and rainbows. It's a very mean and nasty place and I don't care how tough you are it will beat you to your knees and keep you there permanently if you let it. You, me, or nobody is gonna hit as hard as life. But it ain't about how hard ya hit. It's about how hard you can get hit and keep moving forward. How much you can take and keep moving forward. That's how winning is done! Now if you know what you're worth then go out and get what you're worth. But ya gotta be willing to take the hits, and not pointing fingers saying you ain't where you wanna be because of him, or her, or anybody! Cowards do that and that ain't you! You're better than that!"
—Rocky Balboa

People have done far greater things in much less time than I have, but I can honestly say that, for the most part, I gave my all. I guess that's all we can do. Stop paying attention to what everyone else is doing, pick what you want to accomplish, and just do it. Head down, focused, and keeping an eye to the finish line, one step at a time.

It seemed like an impossibility just a few years ago. Not only for hiking the forty-eight, but achieving any large goal for that matter. What a difference a few years can make in a person's life. I learned later in life, comparatively, some of the most important lessons *in* my life. In some ways, it took me until I was almost fifty years old to grow up in some areas, to face some old fears, and to push myself as far as I could (or more accurately) wanted to go.

Here are some of the invaluable lessons taught in achieving a major goal:

- ☐ I needed to hold myself accountable for what I did or didn't do.

- ☐ I'm 100% responsible for my attitude, happiness, future, and my reactions to those around me.

- ☐ Stay hungry, stay focused, and stay humble.

- ☐ Ask for help when you need it.

- ☐ Make it both a challenging but realistic goal.

- ☐ It's hard to compare anything to the feeling of having accomplished a large challenge, and realizing that you were stronger than you thought you were.

Lessons hiking:

- ☐ Most trails that are five miles leading to the summit are magically extended upon descent to seven miles.

- ☐ The rhythm of rock hopping is both invigorating and mentally challenging.

- ☐ Hiking is 49% physical, 51% mental.

- ☐ You can usually smell AT hikers before you can see them.

- ☐ Don't always listen to the exaggerated difficulties of some trails. Respect the difficulties of the trails you thought would be much easier.

☐ Everyone's hike and everyone's journey is different.

My most important lessons learned?

1. Fear is the number one killer of dreams.

2. Every goal or challenge in life must be approached one small step at a time, always moving in a forward, upward, and onward direction.

I can't wait to see what my next fifty years will bring, but until then, I'll continue moving forward, upward, and onward.

Thanks for taking the time to buy and read this book. Independent writers, such as myself, depend on the generosity and patronage of people just like you!

If you have a moment, please take the time to leave a review on Amazon, as reviews play a large role in the overall success of this book.

Chris headed up Mt. Liberty

Eagle sighting at Mt. Cabot
trailhead

The iconic Bondcliff Photo shot

Summit of Waumbek

Mt. Carrigain - Flags on the 48
crew

The view toward Mt. Lafayette

Additional Resources

Here's some additional resources and information you may find helpful in your own White Mountains hiking journey;

Books / Guides;

White Mountain Guide: AMC's Comprehensive Guide to Hiking Trails in the White Mountain National Forest -
by Steven D. Smith (Editor)

AMC's Best Day Hikes in the White Mountains: Four-Season Guide to 60 of the Best Trails in the White Mountains - by Robert N. Buchsbaum (Author)

Guiding / Hiking Educational Services;

Redline Guiding
www.redlineguiding.com
(603) 617-8788

New England Guidebooks and Maps;

The Mountain Wanderer Bookstore
Rt. 112, Lincoln, NH 03251
http://www.mountainwanderer.com

Acknowledgments

I'd like to offer special thanks to all those who have helped me to move upward on the trail, behind the scenes cheering me forward, or simply inspiring me onward to bigger and better things.

Chris Pedersen, Evan Randall, Teri Heatherington, Amy Dalrymple, Suzanne Burke, Cher Gallaugher, Michael Dwyer, Marcia Dana, Joanne Tobey, Jim LaPierre, Mike Boucher, AJ Kubasti, Alex Infantino, Robin Ridener Plumley, Rob Donnelly, Bob & Michelle Taupier, Cory Dupuis, Len Robinson, Joe Ciras, and Randy Pierce.

Special thanks to my Mother and Father for teaching me the love of the outdoors, and the joy that it brings.

Made in the USA
Middletown, DE
20 December 2020